MW00412010

FULL CLASSROOMS
EMPTY SELVES

FULL CLASSROOMS EMPTY SELVES

Reflections on a Decade of Teaching in an American High School

---

Jeremy Adams

Middleman Books, 2012

For more information go to:
www.middlemanbooks.com

ISBN 13: 978-1-475-04510-9
ISBN 10: 1-475-04510-7

Adams, Jeremy
Full Classrooms, Empty Selves: Reflections on a Decade of
Teaching in an American High School - A Memoir / Jeremy
Adams
p. cm.
1. Teaching - High Schoo - California
2. Memoir - Education
3. Adulthood - Parenting - Mentoring

Book Designed by Middleman Book Services

Printed in the United States of America

10 9 8 7 6 5 4 3 2 1

Jeremy Adams's *Full Classrooms, Empty Selves* was the recipient of
the **2012 Middleman Books Boutique Book Award**. As such, all
rights are retained by the author and all royalties from the sales of
this book go to Adams's after cost-recovery.
Go to www. middlemanbooks.com for more information.

For Lauren, Emma, and Benjamin

CONTENTS

Prologue -A Summer's Labor   11

PART I - A METAMORPHOSIS (1995-1999)

My Conversion   34

My Father   63

The Early Temptation   91

Interlude One - A Son Unnamed   119

PART II - REALITY STRIKES (2000-2006)

Standardizing the Extraordinary   128

Zombies & Zealots   158

Interlude Two - "Corn-Cob On The Dog"   181

PART III: SOMETHING'S WRONG IN HERE (2007-)

The Volkslauf   193

A Pedagogy of Propositions   217

Full Classrooms & Empty Selves   235

Interlude Three - A Sand Falls to the Earth   255

PROLOGUE
A SUMMER'S LABOR

Death and taxes are not the only certainties in life if one dares to become a teacher in modern America. A parade of shadowy euphemisms—"cutbacks," "layoffs," "staff reductions"—informs the unfortunate vernacular of the twenty-first century educator.

My wife recently reminded me of this not-so-pleasant reality one morning as we both brushed our teeth at separate sinks. When hearing that my high school district was in the process of making minor layoffs, she wondered aloud what I would do if I couldn't teach.

My job was in no danger, I assured her. Saying it out loud seemed to reassure the both of us.

A few moments passed, along with my wife's anxiety, yet her face suddenly assumed the posture of one who was the recipient of an insight of divine significance.

"Well, you know," she said without making eye contact, "it's great that you have tenure."

I readily agreed. Was there ever anything so apparent in all the world? But something lurked behind her cerebral eyes.

"Why?" I innocently inquired, knowing that our verbal waltz was about to end with a conjugal thud.

"Because you have no skills. I mean if you really think about it, what could you really do for anybody who isn't a student?"

Being told by one's wife that he has "no skills" is never a pleasant experience for any husband. But despite the momentary hurt, I had to admit that she had a point.

I don't have the schooling or credentials to become a lawyer. I don't possess the necessary entrepreneurial spirit to go into commerce or industry. And I certainly am not knowledgeable in the ways of real estate or sales. My two internships during college—one in a K Street Washington, D.C. lobbying firm, the other at a local advertising company—left me with the distinct and lively impression that I needed a job with consequential human contact. I'm never going to thrive in a cubicle, a work pod, or even an office with a picturesque view. I have always needed a job that was not wholly divorced from the prospect of brushing up against occasional moments of enchantment, or even grandeur.

I have had such a job for over a decade.

I am a high school teacher.

Most seminal teacher memoirs are written much later in life, in the sunset of a teacher's career, looking back from afar in the hopes of saying something meaningful and profound about the current state of the classroom or the failings of modern education.

Not this memoir.

The composition of this project begins on the first Monday of summer vacation. It follows the most frustrating year of teaching since I entered the classroom a decade ago. Make no mistake. My teaching corpus is far from complete. Yes, I have taught thousands of students. But I plan to teach thousands more. I have been a teacher long enough to know that I'm no longer a novice or an amateur, yet I'm still far enough away from the splendors of retirement to acknowledge that I still have work aplenty.

But more than that, a decade in the classroom seems like a natural plateau, a place to stop and take stock of not only where I have been, but more importantly, to meditate on where I want to go. Any young teacher can attest to the cynicism that borders on despair emanating from the "veterans" on a school faculty. I witness their shrugs and smirks and offer up a prayer to the teaching gods to spare me their melancholy fate. This memoir is an attempt at immunization, a vain struggle perhaps to inoculate myself from the natural tendency to despair in the twilight of one's teaching career.

Oddly enough, ten years in the classroom is not grounds for the "premature" label of a teacher memoir. A lot can happen in the life of a young teacher in a decade's time. And I'm not simply alluding to education reforms, seismic culture shifts, or the practices of the modern teen. What is disappointing is that no one ever told me that one's twenties are so formative. (Where are all the great, canonical books and films chronicling the *sturm und drang* of being a 26-year old)? Aren't the angst-ridden teenage years or one's libertine college experiences the foundation upon which adulthood rests forever? Yet, it was in my twenties, surrounded by teenagers, that I encountered the true challenge of becoming a man, a self.

At the outset of my career I was the very incarnation of naivety, for I possessed an epic sense of destiny about my ability to be "that one teacher," the teacher so many of us in education can say made a profound difference in our lives. After all, as a teacher in my twenties, I was young enough to remember being in a high school classroom fraught with all the complexities and nuances of being a teenager while at the same time undergoing an adult transformation of my own. True, becoming a husband, a father, or a teacher is categorically different from mastering the skills of being a boyfriend or a student, but at least I could tell these students what lay on their collective horizons. I remembered what it was like to be one of them—hopeful of my future yet vaguely frightened of the world. But I also knew, because I was now in my twenties, how to get past the fear and continue hoping for a life of substance. Having my foot in both epochs of life's journey would be an asset, I wagered.

But this hope never materialized into a reality. At least, not in the way I grandly imagined it would. Lately I have started to notice little things about myself and about the culture in which I teach that don't sit well with me. And so, I'm writing this memoir because something is not quite right about my classroom. At first I assumed that it was I—I am now past thirty and the advantage of being close to their age evaporates as my career progresses. In the last few years something has unsettled me, something more nuanced than the quotidian dreariness of getting older. The simple truth is this: There is a cruel schism between the teacher I am and the teacher I always wanted to be. And just as the conquering of Rome by the barbarians sent Saint Augustine into a philosophic trance for over a decade as he wrote *The City of God*, this realization of my teaching deficiency has sent me into a reflective fury of concern that is the genesis of this memoir.

I have become a weird amalgamation of drill sergeant and Socrates, comedian and paper pusher, motivational speaker and disciplinarian. I have collapsed into a weird admixture of mentor and friend, sometimes cold and distant, sometimes warm and involved. I vacillate depending on the class, the time of year, or the mood of the students. Part of my fluid persona is attributable to trying to be all things to all students. Part of it is an attempt to assuage the diverse number of notions about what a teacher is supposed to be. After a decade in the classroom, it is time to pick a persona. At my best I'm unpredictable in my manner but constant in my commitment. At worst I've become one of those teachers young sophisticates love to scoff at—the guy who takes himself and his craft so seriously that kids quickly get intimidated, or worse, at least for this generation, bored.

I know something is amiss because by the end of every school year I want to amend my teaching persona. I begin every school year with a crystallized mental image of how I want to be viewed, how I hope students will think of me in their minds' eye when exiting my classroom every day. I want to be viewed as eloquent and urbane, eclectically educated, but strangely aloof, even enigmatic. After all, excessive transparency robs the classroom of its rightful aura of potentiality.

I remember a colorful English teacher from my high school years that adeptly used his eccentricity to fuel interest in his class. His name was Slater and his legend on campus was large. We never knew what he was going to say or do. We knew there were vast mental treasures locked away in his mind and we came to class giddily hoping to find delight in what he would reveal to us. His trick was that he never gave away too much of himself to his students. He constantly held back and had us guessing. We didn't know where he attended college. We knew that he hermitically lived on the side of a mountain somewhere but we didn't know exactly which one. He began class one day by announcing that henceforth he no longer wanted to be Mr. Slater; he wanted us to simply

call him "Bob," even if his actual name was "Joe." It was ran-
dom and quirky and, looking back on it, utterly wonderful
for some reason. Mr. Slater, or "Bob," was the central topic
of many a high school lunch while my friends and I tried to
figure out his religious views, his hobbies, and all the minute
facts that define an ordinary human life. It didn't occur to
me until much later that I hung on his every word—not as a
means of unlocking the mysteries of Shakespeare or Milton,
but in the hopes of unlocking the man standing in front of
the classroom.

Ironically, he made himself the center of the learning
experience by not making himself the center of the classroom. And yet, I am nothing like Slater. By the end of the
school year my students are well aware of what I do and do
not know. They know that there is no real difference between
the teacher and the man. I can't help but tell them about
my own educational journey, how it affected my choices in
life, the nexus between learning and life, and how my teachers have informed my answers to the "eternal questions" of
which Dostoevsky writes.

But most of all, my students surely recognize how
woefully ill-equipped I am for classroom failure. What I'm
alluding to is failure of the impenetrable kind, a genus of
failure that cannot be remedied or breached because what
the teacher has to offer a particular student is not what the
student needs at this particular juncture in his/her life. Some
teachers can capture the imaginations of their students
through lively lectures that combine elements of humor,
wit, and curricular content. Others can perplex and charm
through a gentle barrage of Socratic questioning. Many simply scare their pupils into academic submission. The goal,
of course, is to cast the widest didactic web possible in the
hopes of broad success.

But some fish are not meant to be caught by certain

fisherman, no matter how wide, deep or strong the net may be. I remember a student telling me long ago that she simply didn't like my class. When I asked why, she matter-of-factly replied, "I just want to be left alone. Let me decide if this stuff's important. Don't keep telling me it is. That makes you suspicious to me."

Suspicious? The word is haunting.

Ever since this exchange I'm on the lookout for students casting a suspicious eye towards me. I can accept being a bad teacher—but a phony? I have thought about this young lady for many years now. I don't remember her name, her face, or anything else about her except for this simple conversation from early in my teaching career. This student, this Holden Caulfield of the classroom, has come to symbolize a sad acknowledgment that has taken me a decade to make. And this acknowledgement about the natural limitations of the classroom is perhaps the true source of my anxiety.

I can accept the rejection of a subject or a class or even a specific teacher. But when passion evokes suspicion something has gone radically amiss. Indeed, when one considers some of the great historical couplings of teacher and student, there was never any question of suspicion or phoniness, even when tension resonated between them. Plato and Aristotle differed on the nature of reality; just look at Raphael's *School of Athens*. Aristotle clearly would not have approved of Alexander The Great's vainglory. Who knows if Thomas Jefferson and William Small had identical political views? The hostility between Borromini and Bernini was legendary. The magic that transpired between teacher and student, however, was never tainted by the film of suspicion. There is no evidence that the Platonic Academy, the Aristotelian Lyceum, Baroque Rome, or Virginia's William & Mary were epicenters of peaceful intellectual inquiry. Learning can be—perhaps should be—dramatic, even uncomfortable, if it is done correctly.

There was never any doubt that these teachers wanted what all great teachers want: to play a part in the student becoming a better version of him or herself. After all, illumination is not tantamount to indoctrination. Illumination is not a spotlight; it is a mirror of what is possible in oneself.

I always assumed that this noble aspiration was clear to my students. Yes, there are facts, data, and minutia that must be mastered. But the real goal of education is to harness this data in the formation of something beyond banal rote recall, beyond the bubbling in of an answer document. To tell the students what to do with what you've given them is to rob them of the greatest enchantment of an educational journey: the joy of self-discovery. That's why the worst form of teaching is indoctrination. Good teaching is not a watered-down form of intellectual proselytizing. In fact, and ironically, good teaching is sometimes about getting out of the way, letting the text or information work its magic. Teachers are cerebral matchmakers—we introduce students to a variety of ideas, thinkers, and topics and hope that the magic will happen. We facilitate the meeting time and the place and hope mightily for chemistry between the two. We know that the rate of failure is high. After all, how many dates eventually yield a marriage? But if we continually have to explain the relevance of what we teach—if we have to get in the way—then much of the grandeur and enchantment of the classroom is lost.

If I could time travel back to my second year in the classroom, I would carefully listen to what this young lady had to say. But instead of letting her have the last word, I would gently explain that what I teach isn't important because I think that it is. It is important because of what my students can do with their education. I would tell her that it is my job not to leave her alone, that education is not always fun, edifying, or reassuring. I would tell her that the entire point of an education is so none of us ever has to be alone, so we can share in the wisdom of others, so we can share in their pains. To find like minds—minds that share an interest or a curiosity in history or science or drama or whatever—is one of the sublime pleasures of life. Consider Plato's love of Homer's epics, Machiavelli's habit of spending his afternoons immersed in reading the texts of the ancients, Nietzsche's adoration of Montaigne's *Essays*.

For all I know she was having a bad day. Maybe she had quarreled with her parents or a friend. Wherever she is in the world, I'm sure she has no memory of the exchange. But it has stayed with me for the better part of a decade. A better description would be to admit that it has "festered" in me for almost a decade. As I stand on the side of a teaching mountain, safely perched on my reflective plateau, I cannot help but wonder if there are other former students who possess similar opinions. Perhaps she just happened to speak the truth to power. The others who share in her sentiment are happy just to get through the class, to get the credit, to go on with their lives untouched by the many annoyances I have thrown their way. The last thing the typical student wants is a confrontation with a touchy teacher. I can't say I blame them. I wasn't all that different when I was their age. Had my high school teachers cloaked their lectures in the radiant parlance of "enchantment" or "grandeur," I too would have cast a suspicious gaze.

The truth is that I have no aspirations of ever being anything other than a classroom teacher. I graduated from college in June 1998 and was safely ensconced in the bubble of a high school classroom by the next fall. Many of my generational classmates took a year to wander through Europe or work menial jobs so as to maximize their free time. Not only was I back in the high school classroom, but I was in the very same high school I graduated from just four springs earlier.

Bakersfield High School is located in the Central Valley of California and is one of the oldest high schools in California. It boasts more football state championships than any other school in the entire state (we usually don't mention that most of them came in the 1920's). Agriculture and oil dominate the economic landscape of Bakersfield which can be seen in the mascot for Bakersfield High School—The Drillers. (I keep waiting for some clever—or caustic—student to suggest we update the mascot to a greener alternative. Something like the "Turbines" or "Eco-Warriors" would be felicitous). We have a faux oil derrick on campus and an old water tower overlooking the football stadium.

The high school itself is located in the downtown area. Most outsiders would classify Bakersfield High School (BHS) as an "urban" school. It is situated right next to railroad tracks so that when the train cars interlock themselves, the buildings shake as if an earthquake were rocking the school. The school moved to its present location in the early 1900's but had to be rebuilt in the wake of a large earthquake in the 1950's. The football stadium is a real stadium, not dolled-up bleachers. The classrooms have wood paneling and the bookshelves are fitted with glass. The auditorium is one of the finest high school auditoriums west of the Mississippi River and seats well over a thousand people. The local light opera uses our auditorium as its home. The school is so old it served as a fallout shelter during the Cold War. A multitude of stories about ghosts get passed down from class to class. Some of them are rooted in a kernel of truth. Others are merely a phantasmagoria of different tall tales told and retold by faculty who like to prey on the gullibility of fourteen and fifteen year olds. I teach on the top floor of the auditorium. It is a large room that once served as a practice choir room. My blackboards used to have music bars on them before eventually getting replaced by whiteboards. I love the smell of the place when I return to my classroom at the end of every summer. I think it is the residue from the wax the custodians put on the floor in late June.

But the real glory of this place is not rooted in its rich history or even in its *sui generis* appearance. BHS is not just diverse. It is a school that closely parallels the ethnic mosaic that is the melting pot of America *writ large*. And although the melting pot metaphor is no longer fashionable to most of the American intelligentsia, it is wholly appropriate when describing the culture and environment of BHS. White, Black, and Latino students each constitute a healthy block of the school population. If ever there was an ideal microcosm of racial integration, cultural pluralism, and socio-economic diversity, it is Bakersfield High School.

My Advanced Placement classes have students who are black and white, rich and poor, valedictorians and students taking their first advanced class. My students thoroughly understand the meaning of America's creed as encapsulated by its former national motto—*E Pluribus Unum*—because they live the ideal everyday. Learning how to interact with those who don't look like you or think like you is an essential ingredient in any meaningful education in America. And while this particular virtue of the school will never be observable through test scores or a school ranking, it is for this reason that the high school commands an extraordinary degree of fidelity from its alumni. It is in such a setting that my students learn that the idea of America—its civic faith if you will—is grounded in an eternal optimism about the power of human agency to forge a world in accordance with civilization's highest aspirations, a uniquely American belief that freedom is a necessary prerequisite for living a life of meaning and genuine significance. The right to pursue this end on one's own terms, to encounter difficulties in life with a freedom to either fight or flee, is the core of our creed as a people.

It would require a raconteur with wondrous powers of description to appropriately describe the level of affection I and countless others have for this place. When the concept of community is evoked, most people usually get a fuzzy mental image in their minds of an America from the 1950's or before—an America of block parties, bowling leagues and the like. I would never know the splendors of what it means to be a fixture in a real community had I not come to work at this extraordinary place. To be a single link in the chain of a place so filled with history and legend is a pleasure that can only be described as sublime. My four siblings attended the school. I attended it. My father taught here for almost twenty years. In truth, it is the only professional home I've ever known. It is the only one I hope to know. There is a stronger sense of community among the students, faculty, and parents than in any other setting I have ever encountered. Alumni proudly proclaim "Once a Driller, Always a Driller." Every school makes the claim of somehow being special. Most people in the Bakersfield community would readily admit that the long and glorious history of the place creates a narrative that makes it easier to command the affections of incoming and graduating students. Most students would tell you that the animating virtue of the school is pride: pride in the history and pride in the possibility of more glory. This is the school that boasts alumni such as Earl Warren (Chief Justice of the Supreme Court) and Frank Gifford (famous football player). It is the oldest high school in the county, having begun its history in 1893.

I am not sure if my teaching troubles—suspicious students, shifting personas, an aging classroom demeanor—are timeless or particular to my generation. Therefore, it makes little sense to morph this memoir into an homage to the

past. I haven't been teaching long enough to be nostalgic for
a bygone era. My neophyte status robs me of any historical
omniscience in the area of education. I have no intimate
knowledge of the "brain gap" of the Sputnik years. I didn't
take part in the argument that students had become unimag-
inative in the late 1960's, mere participants in an elaborate
process of mass regurgitation. I was not an apostle of E.D.
Hirsch's call for emphasizing cultural literacy in the 1980's.

If there is any part of American society that appears to
be in constant crisis, however, it is surely education. And
it is here that I depart from my own teaching travails and
note a very different form of teaching distress. Rarely a year
passes when the state of the classroom does not grace the
cover of *Time* or *Newsweek* with the same redundant sto-
ryline that American education is in need of major reform,
that a stentorian effort is required to correct a crisis in the
making. Such supercilious suggestions, of course, are not
without some merit. But this is precisely why experienced
teachers approach each new educational movement with
a shrug of wariness and an attitude of dread. If one were
to follow the hysteria of magazine covers and newspaper
headlines, the frequency of the need for revolution in education would make even the likes of Mao or Lenin blush. Why
invest oneself too much in the next education revolution
when you know you are going to be swept away in the next
one a few years later?

If ever there was a segment of American life that followed Jefferson's dictum that there ought to be revolution every twenty years or so, it is certainly public education. If the
classroom is the laboratory of democratic renewal and the
nursery for future economic vitality, the ever-changing nature of the world requires perennial experimentation and innovation in the classroom. As America's economic evolution
continues its arch from agriculture to industry, from goods

and services to technology, American students must continually enhance their skill-set in an interconnected, globalized economy. We teachers "get it." We understand our role; John Dewey's pragmatism continues to cast a tall shadow on the modern classroom. We understand that any social engineering, both good and bad, begins in the classroom.

What baffles most sensible teachers, however, is the willful ignorance about the proper role of the school in a democratic society. It is on this point, appropriately, that the wisdom of the teaching veterans—yes, the same ones who shrug and smirk with great frequency and fanfare at teacher meetings—is prescient. I sympathize with their view that no government program or new teaching modality will ever replace the majestic foundations that can be laid by involved parents, passionate teachers, or curious students. Is there any possible panacea that would cure the problems propagated by a prurient culture, an entitlement mentality, or uninvolved parents? There is only one conversation policy-makers seem to enjoy. It is the same conversation Socrates has with Glaucon when postulating the ideal society in *The Republic*. It is a conversation that posits education as both the hand-maiden and the elixir of a splendid political vision, a utopian notion of what can occur when civilization embraces a muscular educational vision of universal access and excellence. This is a topic ripe with the potential for grandiloquence. Political leaders can eschew reality in order to rhetorically muse about the utopian vision that can be ushered into a reality with a universally well-educated generation. Such speeches can give a litany of benign social and economic impacts, from increases in worker productivity to a broadening of the American middle class. It can be claimed that education can serve as an elixir to all of our social pathologies, from addiction and dropouts, to racial inequality and anxieties about international challenges.

The other conversation we should be having, the one that makes a daily impact on every classroom in America, is not how education ideally affects society, but how society affects the classroom. This is the conversation politicians and policy-makers avoid at all costs because it concerns a pathology for which they have no prescription. Social ills and cultural blemishes do more than simply make a passive appearance in the classroom. These ills and blemishes, on the other hand, are not the stuff of high oratory or soaring Platonic theory. Nobody wants to talk about a generation that is so bombarded with stimulation of all kinds, from cell phones to iPods, that a properly functioning classroom appears static and dormant. Who wants to mention the difficulty of teaching students whose own parents often explain away their bad habits; it doesn't matter if it is cutting class, cheating, or poor test performance.

Outsiders to the culture of modern education are quick to argue that these observations amount to nothing more than highfalutin whining, that fixing broken homes and altering learning dispositions falls beyond the purview of curricular guidelines and education reform. Teachers must teach no matter the external reality of the world beyond their classroom doors. Bashing the American education system is so systemically a part of American discourse that it's become a national pastime akin to hating Congress or complaining about the evils of high energy prices. Clichés and platitudes about America's failing education system figure in every election cycle. And just as we were once told about the Soviet Union's science advantage in the 1950's or Japan's economic superiority in the 1980's, we are now inundated with the drab reality that the rest of the world is catching up. We educators are told that, in a globalized economy predicated on knowledge and technology, the only reservoir of hope lies in producing a dynamic generation of highly skilled laborers.

And this is true. But what is interesting to observe is how consistent American education has been in meeting these challenges over the past one-hundred years. High schools were created over a century ago to empower and enhance the skills of young people to succeed in an economy transitioning from agrarianism to industrialization. It is extraordinary that an education system that has supposedly been in continual crisis for forty years somehow helped to win the Cold War, laid the groundwork for the technological and information revolution and produced the most dynamic workforce in the world.

Not bad for a "broken" system.

But I am no apologist. I am no scholar on educational trends or international comparisons. I don't do research and the only "sample" I understand with clerical certainty is the sample sitting in my classroom on a daily basis. What I have is a hope, an inspiration, a steady prayer of mattering to those whom I teach.

No matter how difficult the school year proves to be, I still have high hopes for the future of my classroom. I have never been anything but a teacher. This was not, of course, my ultimate ambition as a young man. Like so many young people with a scintilla of talent or achievement, I conceived of a life that escaped the monotony of bills, children, and conventional professions. But now that I am a teacher, there is little I wouldn't do to remain here forever. By the middle of July I begin to feel jittery and on edge. I have a limited capacity for amusing myself. I feel myself getting sucked back into the enchanting vortex of a high school classroom as summer's twilight approaches. I'm the teacher who is secretly terrified of reaching the age when students and colleagues begin to collectively ask me about my retirement plans.

But retirement is the last thing on my mind this summer. It has taken ten years for me to admit that, at its core, teaching is actually a quasi-religious craft. There is a great deal of faith that is necessary for one to believe that he/she is actually doing the work of the education gods. Teachers must work their entire lives for an outcome they will neither see nor know. A teacher's work is not measurable by the conventional yardsticks of success. Money? Don't get me started. Power? Only of a very indirect sort. Respect? Who knows what my students are really thinking?

In fact, the yardstick of classroom success is so infinitely vague that only a teacher of great faith could believe in the majesty or utility of his/her work. Doctors witness the power of their healing. Lawyers listen to verdicts from judges and clients. Artists have a canvas to look back upon with pride or distress. Writers can peruse the aisle of a local bookstore. They can all collectively point and say:

"There! That patient or client or painting or book bears the mark of my efforts. If I were to die today there would be a reminder, a residue, of what I worked to achieve."

But for teachers the mark of our toil is ambiguous. The occasional student will write a kind note or shake your hand while uttering an encouraging word or two. As teachers, these are the moments we live for. We bask in the momentary glow of doing our jobs well, at least for this student, at least for this moment in time. Our faith seems justified. But then years pass. We never hear from the student who wrote us the kind note or shook our hand. Our faith begins to waiver as we ask the hardest of all questions: how can the influence of any teacher be measured in the context of another human being's life?

These are self-indulgent musings, I fully admit. But if a person is to love what he does and cherishes the possibilities it promotes, then conjuring a yardstick for success is not unreasonable. I cannot help but feel, however, that my longing for such a yardstick marks a man who has lost a little faith in the enterprise of education. Faith in education does not require divine revelation, burning bushes or even outward affirmation by one's students. But it does demand hope. It demands patience. It asks teachers to venture to the water's edge at the outset of every school year to throw a hundred or so pebbles into the water in the hopes of making some waves on the contours of history. The torture is not knowing which pebbles make the waves and which pebbles sink to the bottom. I have seen very few waves in my decade in the classroom. Perhaps this is from a lack of patience, or worse, a loss of faith.

I am told by my older colleagues that the waves are out there. You can tell these old-timers have faith in the fecundity of their efforts. I know that most of them don't see any waves, either. But it doesn't seem to faze them. They know the waves are out there. They just know it. In this knowledge these teachers are exemplars of the teaching faith. In the wake of these conversations with veteran teachers, I am always left to wonder: can I throw the pebbles any further?

On the last day of every school year, the retirees sit in front of the faculty during an after school meeting. The school choir proceeds to serenade them. It's a nice gesture. But there is something I find violently putrid about it. I always watch the retirees closely and wonder to myself, "How will I possibly meet that moment when it comes for me?"

There are a great many things I hope to feel when the class of 2039 raises its voice in tribute to my forty years of teaching. I hope I'm not sad. I hope I'm ready to go on to other things. I will surely be thinking of the dozens of friends I acquired throughout my career who retired or passed away long ago. But I also hope that I can say my life meant something to someone other than myself. A man labors in front of a classroom five hours a day for forty years. How can he not hope that he understands what it all adds up to in the end? The Scottish Enlightenment thinker David Hume once explained that "solitude is misery." I hope that when I transition from the communal existence of the classroom to the solitary living of a retiree that I harbor no regrets. I hope that I can prove Mr. Hume wrong. Most of all, I hope that the forty years of ordinary teaching will translate into an extraordinary life of significance.

But before that can happen, there are a few things I have to get off my chest about the last ten years.

After a decade in the classroom, it is not difficult to daydream, to consider where all of my students are, to imagine what it is they are doing with themselves. For some I already know, and the results are as diverse as the personalities I encounter everyday. I have former students in Iraq; students who have become teachers in Europe and in at-risk communities; students attending Yale Law School. But I also have students who are working at the local mini-mart; students who got pregnant or got someone pregnant their first year out of high school; students who were seduced by drugs and alcohol because they couldn't handle the responsibility of being away from home. In my ever-widening pool of former students, there is surely a representative that reflects every flavor on the vast palate of post-secondary possibilities. I am writing this memoir because I doubt I did for my students all that I could have done. I didn't throw the pebbles far enough. I write in the hopes that my next thirty years as a teacher are equally magnificent or better than the first ten.

I write hoping to recapture that ineffable something that led me to the classroom a decade ago.

I write to renew.

After all, to teach is to have something to say. To teach is to matter to those who are learning. To teach is to sew

oneself into the fabric of the lives you are attempting to improve.

PART I
A METAMORPHOSIS (1995 – 1999)

CHAPTER I
MY CONVERSION

His nickname was "The Axe."

We got off to a rough start my freshman year of college when he told me that I was "intellectually constipated."

And yet, there is not a day that passes when I do not think of this extraordinary man. To those who know him, his titanic influence lends itself to easy hyperbole and endless superlatives; to those who have never experienced the full weight of his artistry, any testimony I offer is likely to trigger disbelief. A truly accurate account of his genius must be left to those of like mind—academics, scholars, fellow connoisseurs of high erudition. I, on the other hand, was only his pupil; any knowledge I now have of him is remembered through the subjective prism of awe.

My odyssey to his classroom began the previous December. I was working at a Christmas tennis camp my senior year of high school when my father suddenly appeared on the court holding an envelope high in the air. The sky was dark London-gray with fog that was stubborn to recede. This was fairly typical meteorological cuisine for Bakersfield in the middle of December, yet he enigmatically wore sunglasses. I told the five-year-olds who could barely hold a racquet, the ones we affectionately called "small fries," to sit down on the tennis court for just a minute. I had to find out if my life was about to change.

"Awfully thin," he cynically intoned.

I calmly grabbed it out of his hand, feigning indifference to his sardonic commentary. I turned my back to him and started walking towards the net. I knew exactly what it was. It was the letter I had been waiting for since first stepping on the campus of Washington & Lee University the previous June. My mother, father and I had taken a trip to the East Coast that mirrored the journey thousands of West Coast teenagers make with their parents. We looked at a variety of schools in Virginia, New York and Pennsylvania. My father insisted we write down our top four choices before the trip. He wanted to compare this list to the one we would make after concluding our visitations.

While we disagreed about second and third place, by the end of the trip there was unanimous consensus that my ideal school was Washington & Lee University. W&L, as members of its community and alumni affectionately call it, is located in the heart of Virginia's Shenandoah Valley in a small town named Lexington. Lexington, Virginia sits at the intersection of I-64 and I-81 and is steeped in history, especially of the Southern variety. George Washington's donation helped to keep the school open in its early days and Robert E. Lee served as the school's president in the wake of the Civil War after refusing more than five thousand other job offers. Lee is buried on the campus (in "Lee Chapel," of course) and his most enduring legacy is his implementation of the honor code and speaking traditions. W&L is immediately next door to the Virginia Military Institute, which boasts that Stonewall Jackson was once on staff and that George Marshall is its most famous alumnus.

The attraction of W&L to this Southern California kid had little to do with its proximity to Southern history or culture. When I was a teenager, I never related to grown men who participated in Civil War reenactments (it always seemed a little goofy and creepy to me; an example of history buffs who were perhaps a tad too enthusiastic about their intellectual pursuits) nor did I possess a flowering appreciation for Antebellum America. Many an aspiring student has been seduced by the aesthetic of a college campus. I loved the California campuses of Berkeley, UCLA and Occidental. But this place was unlike any I had ever visited. The campus stands aloft a hill à la the Greek acropolis and its mellifluous white columns and dashing red brick project a power and a presence that all other college campuses can only hope to duplicate or shadow. Yet it was more than aesthetic beauty or historical gravitas that I detected that day.

What was mysterious about my visit on that June afternoon was the stentorian desolation of the campus, barren of not just human beings but movement of any kind. Instead of casting an ominous shadow over us, the stillness of the campus imbued the moment with a piercing sense of intimacy— an intimacy that remains with me fifteen years later.

Most of my students long to attend a university in an urban setting, preferably Los Angeles, San Francisco, or San Diego. This preference, of course, has nothing to do with education and everything to do with the maximization of social outlets. (Think bars, beaches, and every indolent venue imaginable). The prospect of four years in a small mountain hamlet is anathema to the sensibilities of most

modern college-goers. Most of my students do not understand what I learned on the day of my visit to W&L; to study
and think in the hustle and bustle of a cosmopolitan setting
is to miss the best time in life to withdraw from the celerity
of a modern existence. The arduous nature of education isn't
found in the reading, writing, or discussing, but in the thinking. Thought—real thought, not the shallow cerebral froth
yielded from leisurely musings—is the byproduct of time
and silence, neither of which is in abundant supply in urban
settings. When undertaking the serious business of becoming educated, an aesthetic aphrodisiac such as the Blue Ridge
Parkway isn't the worst companion in the world.

I have long since given up trying to explain the majesty
of this place to my beach-bound students. To them, campus
beauty is at best a convenient distraction from the arduousness of college, not a necessary ingredient in its completion.
Socrates would agree with my students, of course. One
cannot hold a dialogue with a river, a tree, or an overgrown
pasture, Socrates would say. What is necessary in Socratic
education is not solitude but propinquity. I suppose living
for four years in Virginia suffused a bit of the Jeffersonian in
me because on this occasion I must dissent from my Greek
hero. There is an unspeakable fusion that takes place within
a student between the aesthetic beauty of his surroundings
and the task of reading dense texts and thinking high-minded thoughts. Walking the empty grounds of W&L on that
beautiful June afternoon was perhaps the first time I grasped
an essential truth about the power and poignancy of beauty.
True beauty does not elicit a passive response, it lures like a
siren. It resonates in the chest of the observer with such ferocity that the observer wants to be one with the beauty—be
it a sunset, a symphony, or the simplicity of a college campus.

The three of us wandered the campus gazing at the co-
lonial architecture, each cloaked in silence, each hoping that

we were not isolated in our unbounded exhilaration. And just as trees bend their branches to maximize their exposure to the light, so too was I willing to change all that I had known to saturate the rays of this place. Six months later I opened up a thin envelope on a foggy California morning to learn that I had won early admittance to the college of my dreams. My father already knew the verdict, of course. He had taken a gigantic flashlight to the back of the envelope and saw but a single word at the top of the letter: "Congratulations."

I wanted to attend Washington & Lee because I conceived of the place as a slingshot to greater things. From the time I was a child, there was an unspoken trajectory—a silent paternal pact between father and son—my life was supposed to travel on.

"Excellence in all things" was supposed to produce a life that mattered, that achieved, that laid the foundation for a life defined by greatness. As an ambitious and cocky eighteen-year-old, I never really considered what constituted "greatness" or even "achievement," for that matter. What mattered to me was that I was on a trajectory towards achieving them. My favorite Teddy Roosevelt quote comes to mind as I recall the life I once imagined for myself: "It is not the critic who counts; not the man who points out how the strong man stumbles, or where the doer of deeds could have done them better. The credit belongs to the man who is actually in the arena, whose face is marred by dust and sweat and blood; who strives valiantly…" It was almost as if my life were an already-formed connect-the-dot figure that simply required me to go through the motions of connecting the dots: get into a good school, get a good GPA, go to law school, next dot, next dot, next dot. I was no different from the other tens of thousands of young people who enter America's highly-esteemed universities waiting to connect

their dots. We are soldiers in an army of utilitarian learners, ready to tackle new challenges of the college classroom
in the hopes of bolstering our resumes. And although many
of us who attended these universities would never speak
these words, we did feel that we were meant for great things.
There is an intuitive impulse that whispers to us that we are
somehow significant.

    I remember taking a keen interest in the 1992 Presiden-
tial election between George H.W. Bush and Bill Clinton. At
sixteen I wasn't sure why it mattered to me who won, but it
did. I recall sitting at a park in my car reading my US History textbook and listening to the radio as they announced
Clinton's victory. That summer I began reading some books
by Bob Woodward and even took to reading the occasional
political magazine. I herald from a very conservative town
in the central valley of California where the election of Bill
Clinton was met with about as much excitement as I am sure
Ronald Reagan's was in Berkeley twelve years earlier. My interest in the political process was nothing more than a minor
interest, slowly evolving toward an end I could not imagine
at the time. I wasn't particularly partisan nor did I know
enough about political ideology to be ideological. I knew
Democrats liked to tax and that my parents were lukewarm
Republicans who didn't much care for Reagan (something
about depriving teachers of their Social Security) but loved
his vice-president. I didn't participate in any protests, walk-
outs or lock-ins. This middle-class scion of two successful public school teachers wasn't outraged about much. It
should come to no surprise that my interest in politics still
paled in comparison to my passions for tennis and music. If
I had to choose between Bush winning the White House and
Boris Becker winning Wimbledon, there would have been no
contest. There was no revelatory moment of being moved by
an MLK or touched by a Kennedy, just a meandering interest

in the politics of my time.

By the time I entered college my freshman year, politics was the only possible major I could imagine. Science and math were nonplus. I had yet to find any enchantment in reading (my father would label me a 'philistine') so most of the humanities were unappealing. I remember sitting with my advisor for the first time. For some odd reason I had worn a coat and tie to the meeting. He told me that I should start off in a political philosophy class. I wasn't pleased with the suggestion. I wanted to learn about "real politics." Give me a class on the presidency or foreign policy or something entrenched in the "real world." Bob Woodward probably didn't give a damn about Plato's *Allegory of the Cave* or the radicalism of Lycurgus. Why should I? My advisor told me that I would get to the "pragmatic stuff" soon enough. He looked at the class schedule and sat back in his chair looking slightly confused.

"I'm not entirely sure who's teaching the course but it's a good place to start."

Upon further investigation I learned that this class was normally taught by a professor on the brink of retirement. His nickname was "Easy D" and you can imagine what the "D" stood for. The only "D" I ever received was in handwriting when I was in the 5th grade. The prospect of a "D" in college was a harrowing notion to a young man whose father was working three extra jobs to pay the tuition.

The first day of this political philosophy course looked nothing like any introductory class most of my current students will ever know. Most of them go to public California universities where introductory classes of five hundred students or more are not uncommon, where a professor is merely a talking speck in front of the lecture hall. I am fortunate enough to also teach classes at the university level on an adjunct basis and can personally attest to large classes.

This political philosophy classroom, on the other hand, looked nothing like the typical lecture hall with stadium seating that always reminds me of a miniaturized version of the Hollywood Bowl. Instead, it was rectangular in shape and had one long boardroom table in the middle of it. Clearly, this was a place for discussions, not lectures, a place for intellectual intimacy instead of personal anonymity. There were about fifteen students instead of five hundred and I already knew that an absence would definitely be noticed. I sat next to a new friend I had just made the previous weekend during the infamous W&L freshmen swim test.

This was the first college class I would ever sit through. Why, I wondered, did it have to be with a professor nicknamed "Easy D?" I sat waiting for Easy D to arrive. Everyone else in the class bristled with confidence. To my astonishment, a man in his early thirties sporting a Snoopy tie walked into the classroom. At first I couldn't tell his national or ethnic background. I later learned that he had grown up in South America. He had short curly black hair and wore glasses with strikingly small lenses. Clearly, this was not Easy D.

In fact, this is the man who changed my life, the one who saved me from my shallow and sophomoric view of life, the one who resisted giving me the easy answers to the difficult questions of life, the one who illuminated for me the enormous stakes that should be involved in any educational sojourn.

Of course, I didn't know this at the time. I was just relieved it wasn't Easy D regally sitting at the head of the table. Sitting there on that fall afternoon, I had no desire to be changed or molded into something finer that what I already was. At eighteen, I had yet to make the existential dichotomy between a real and an accidental life or ponder the aspirations of human completeness and spiritual longing.

I had yet to experience a crisis of belief because I didn't know what I believed. Like all great teachers, this young professor was not about to give away the answers to the important questions.

My appreciation of what he was trying to do for his students was slow to evolve. The fall of 1994 was this professor's first year at W&L in a tenure-track position. His educational odyssey had taken him from the west coast campus of UC Santa Barbara to the legendary University of Chicago, where some of the greatest minds of his field had worked. I had never heard of Leo Strauss, Allan Bloom, Saul Bellow or the famous Committee on Social Thought. In short, I didn't know enough to be impressed. We were both freshmen of a very different sort. And although the students in the class had both brains and ambition, none of us were initially ready to embrace the vulnerability his teaching demanded of us.

Vulnerability or Socratic ignorance ranked high on this professor's hierarchy of necessary virtues if one is to experience the weight of his class as a fully transformative event. My vulnerability was foisted upon me, however, with the delicacy of a vituperative child throwing a temper tantrum in the crib. I wanted none of it, at first. After all, Aristotle, De Tocqueville and Madison are fine, but I wanted to get to "real learning," the flesh of the political world, not its esoteric skeleton. I wanted to discuss Clinton and Bush, not Cicero and Boethius. A few weeks into the class, the professor made a proposal I would never forget.

He generously offered to read drafts of our first papers if we were prompt enough to turn them in a few days before the final due date. Two or three weeks into my first term, I had found his class interesting and intimidating as hell. But I still had my shield on. I was still far from vulnerable. In my embryonic mental state I understood the class to be a conventional survey course of political thinkers. As yet, I had failed to grasp the introspective nobility—perhaps necessity—of the subject matter at hand.

He announced to the class that all drafts would be in his outbox later that day. I made the mistake of stopping by his office on the way to dinner that evening to pick up my rough draft, eagerly anticipating some small changes. As I removed my paper from his outbox I was not sure if what I picked up was my rough draft. My doubt sprouted from the fact that of the ten or so sentences on the first page only one remained. Almost all of my words had been crossed out (violently, it seemed) by lines ending with curly Q's at the end of them. As if universal rejection of my prose were not enough, he had taken the liberty of adding Post-It notes all over the first and second pages to give additional critiques of my shoddy performance. At the end of his comments he wrote, with the utmost of brio, that it was clear I was "intellectually constipated."

Unless the cafeteria was serving Apricot Glazed Pork Loin, I never missed a meal. Now I couldn't even eat dinner.

My initial response was both simple and juvenile: "What an asshole!"

I took this annihilation of my first paper as an episode of academic hazing. If my paper had been a battlefield, a nuclear device had been detonated on it. Virtually nothing was left of the original paper. Perhaps, I thought, this was an experience every W&L freshman was supposed to have in the hopes of inspiring awe and approbation for the professors. Maybe there is an unspoken and unofficial code for professors teaching freshmen courses. But this preliminary assessment of the situation was nowhere close to correct. When the final papers were graded I received a "B-." Not bad, and it could have been much worse. What struck me about the entire episode was that he had originally given me a "C+" and erased it. It wasn't hard to discern the erased

grade buried underneath the higher grade. I have long pon-
dered his reasoning for erasing the lower grade. I have since
gone back and re-read the final paper I submitted. I would
certainly have deserved the "C" or even lower. I would like
to think that he saw in me a sliver of what he knew I could
become, that although I was still an apostle of utilitarian
learning, there was hope for those with willing hearts and
open minds.

I got better at reading the difficult texts as the fall wore
on. I perfected my thesis statements, mastered my syntax,
and learned to use the texts as guides of my own thinking. I
also got to know the professor on a more personal basis. For
all its beauty and complexity of character, the greatest catalyst for authentic student learning at W&L is that the place
fosters and forges deep relationships between the faculty and
the students. An impactful conversation with a professor is
as likely to take place at a fraternity dinner or, in my case, a
tennis court, as in a classroom. We played tennis together,
off and on, during my tenure at W&L. The Axe finally beat
me the final time we ever played my senior year as my tennis skills atrophied from their freshman year peak. After
we shook hands, I remember telling him that he didn't have
to mention my defeat to anyone. His reply was classic Axe:
"Oh, I'm going to enjoy this for a while."

In my decade as a teacher I have learned that conversations between pupils and teachers are more memorable for
the pupil. Those conversations on the W&L tennis courts
are amongst the most formative I have ever had with another human being. To The Axe, I am sure, there was nothing memorable about them. We talked about what it means
to really read a book; about the dozen or so times he had
read Hobbes' *Leviathan*; about my need to devote a summer
reading Adam Smith's *The Theory of Moral Sentiments*. I
also told him some of my own fears and personal opinions.

I told him that I have always feared, and still do, that when I die it will be slow and painful. (Why in the world I told him this I will never know). I told him that, although I was no expert, I thought his level of grandiloquence with words could pave the road to a highly successful writing career if he ever wanted to popularize a highly academic subject. And he was the first one in the W&L community to call me in to his office my senior year to ask how I was doing in the wake of my sister's unexpected death. He surely knew I was not the most gifted of students. Yet he was a perfect mentor for someone of my sensibilities—firm in his expectations, but encouraging enough to hope. As erudite and classically educated as The Axe was, I was always surprised to hear the same pop advice from him over and over again: "Never Say Die!" There are schemes of grandeur that await those who learn to let go of the fear of confusion or failure. You can't show these schemes to others. You can only discover them for yourself. He waited for me to make my own discoveries with gentle nudges and timely critiques, having faith that my mind would eventually ripen, yielding treasures of the mind that remain with me to this day.

When the class concluded, the most extraordinary, if unexpected, thing happened to me. The texts and the discussions stayed with me. I kept retuning to them in my own mental wanderings as if they were now somehow essential to my understanding of the world. I saw a linkage between Aristotle's view of the family and the social pathologies of America's inner-cities. I used Lycurgus to better understand equality, Pericles to understand liberty. Madison's theories in the *Federalist Papers* now illuminated the behavior of political interest groups.

Just as priests are sometimes defrocked of their ecclesiastic authority when losing their faith or straying from dogma, so too had I lost my power to defend my utilitarian

faith of learning. Education, I now understood by way of
The Axe, nourished much more than just career aspirations.
This isn't to say that I had lost my ambitious and competitive
nature. But it had been transformed into something finer
than raw narcissism. For the first time I understood Rousseau's chosen motto: *vitam impendere vero* (Consecrating
One's Life to the Truth) and looked upon it with more than
a shallow nod of thunderstruck intrigue. I now began to
question the value of all that I had come to worship: power
without purpose, trivial possession, impersonal popularity.
There was something more real, more desperate about this
radical approach to learning.

I was suddenly hungry for more.

During my first Virginia winter, my hunger for learning
became ravenous. While I have always been relatively social,
for the first time that semester I began to cherish a solitude
nourished by books. The more I withdrew the more majestic
my life seemed to become. I felt more alive reading Seneca
or listening to Wagner than throwing a football or watching
a movie. I opened every book with the distinct impression
that on any page, in any chapter, something may be written
that would change my life. I discovered in the course of my
studies that my new disposition was not particularly odd.
Thoreau escaped to Walden to live a more Spartan-like existence. Mahler roamed the hills and mountains of his youth
with a religious reverence for their power. Kierkegaard
broke off an engagement with his fiancé, Regina, because
he wanted to devote himself to his intellectual pursuits. In
no way am I comparing myself to their genius. But finding
pleasure in the solitude of one's own reflections was a new
sensation to me. It is a pleasure that provides the foundation
for a nobler form of life than I had ever known or imagined.

What happened to me was not all that different from
the metamorphosis the military evokes in basic training: I

was stripped of my former being in the hopes of rebuilding my life into something beyond the rudimentary construct of a youthful self. This youthful self—my former being—was the ontological equivalent of a cosmic roulette wheel, the by-product of an infinite number of impersonal forces beyond my control. Whether the ball ends up on black or red, odd or even, 1-36, or double zero is as controllable as determining when one will be born, who one's parents will be, where one will live, or one's genetic code. There are innumerable components of one's ultimate identity that are stealthily crafted by the forces of Chance. This is what the ancients labeled an "accidental existence." Socratic wisdom is the acknowledgment that one's mind is largely the consequence of this cosmic roulette wheel. The first step in overcoming such a dreary deterministic world-view in the hopes of achieving a "real existence" is to acknowledge the role that chance has played in the formation of the self. To empower reason to make such a dashing admission is to begin the process of self-actualization. When Socrates was asked where he was from he did not say Athens. He said, "The World." Athens is what the roulette wheel gave him. The world is what he conquered with his mind, his questioning, in a word, his philosophizing. A real existence escapes the mundane and banal. It escapes Athens in the hopes of understanding the world. It seeks out and favors the more encompassing issues that are the stuff of authentic learning. A real existence is genuinely annoyed by the everydayness of life.

What I believe The Axe wanted from me, what he wanted from all of his students, was to realize that we can all partake in a higher form of living through the magic of the classroom. Different people can disagree about what constitutes this higher form, but at least we should think about what it individually means for us. A teacher must not teach the primacy of one world-view over the other. A good teacher—one who cherishes self-discovery—simply makes students aware of the options and the stakes involved. To be immune to the concerns of God and The Good, to ignore questions of justice and unfairness, to close one's eyes to the contents and possibilities of virtue and happiness is to stay ignorantly tethered to life's roulette table. And while everydayness occupies us, it doesn't have to define us. An artist might find a higher form of living in the creative powers of the paintbrush that mimic the physical world. A scientist discovers it by partaking in an objective quest for empirical knowledge. A soldier finds it through the ethic of glory and courage. And the examples could go on *ad infinitum.*

Perhaps the greatest lesson I learned from The Axe is that true wisdom does not necessarily consist of answers. True knowledge consists of knowing the correct questions. True knowledge is a disposition, not merely a cerebral stockpile of highfalutin information. It masks a faux wisdom that is always cloaked in the shadows of subjective tastes and preferences. A disposition to question first, to always be open to the prospect of refining one's most cherished convictions provides a bulwark against the seductions of quick convictions and prosaic knowledge. It was said of Socrates that he was the ugliest man in Athens, a fact that he himself was proud of. How appropriate that the ugliest man in Athens, a man whose outer features merited such aesthetic ribbing, cared so little about the slight (or the ridicule given to him by Aristophanes in *The Clouds*). He even bragged about it. What mattered to him was not the illusionary world of external impressions but the real reflection of one's inner being.

To chisel this inner being into something worthy of a human being, however, is to always question. Questions linger, questions stay with us, questions always avail themselves of reformation in the hopes of inching closer to the truth of an issue. But this process of questioning retains a brutal

gloss to it. It can be more than uncomfortable. To put away
the umbrella of one's youth that has always served as a protective buffer against the doubts of the world can be the most
disorienting of activities. Of all the habits of the mind that I
try to encourage in my students this one is the most resisted.
It is always more pleasant to watch a news channel that rein-
forces our political prejudices than one that challenges them.
It is easier for a Christian to read C.S. Lewis than Friedrich
Nietzsche. How often do we merely read the newspaper
columnists we already agree with? Sitting in a choir that is
being preached to is quite pleasurable if it allows us to stay
in the only mental cocoon we have ever known. It might
be pleasurable, but it doesn't lead a student to intellectual
growth. To find pleasure in an adversarial mind, to trace the
contours of an idea or work one finds repulsive or just plain
wrong is the true mark of a mind that has achieved something mature and noteworthy. An eloquent mind never has
time for restlessness and despair, for it longs to be nourished
by the wisdom and ideas of education. Routines, schedules,
and ordinariness are facts of life, but they don't have to be
our method of living. Continuous education and mindful
questioning offer a way out. This, I think, was Rainer Maria
Rilke's point as he advised his young correspondent in *Letters
to a Young Poet*:

> You are so young, so before all beginning,
> and I want to beg you, as much as I can, to be
> patient toward all that is unsolved in your heart
> and to try to love the questions themselves like
> locked rooms and like books that are written in
> a very foreign tongue. Do not seek the answers,
> which cannot be given you because you would
> not be able to live them. And the point is, to live
> everything. Live the questions now. Perhaps

you will then gradually, without noticing it, live
along some distant day into the answer.

I readily admit that these are the ruminations of someone with a decidedly enthusiastic bent towards the liberal
arts. One of the consequences of my metamorphosis from
utilitarian learning to liberal arts learning was that I fell in
love with reading. To encounter in genius—be it a philosopher, an artist, or a scientist—an expression that one can
adopt as one's own is the height of the extraordinary. What's
even greater, still, is the possibility of encountering in genius
what one has already considered for oneself. As Emerson
notes in *Self-Reliance*: "A man should learn to detect and
watch that gleam of light which flashes across his mind from
within, more than the lustre of the firmament of bards and
sages. Yet he dismisses without notice his thought, because it
is his."

These are pleasures I was adamantly unaware of before college, before my conversion away from the utilitarian
covenant of learning. A liberal arts education, at its core, is
the education of men and women possessing freedom. The
question of what one should do with freedom is the central
question in a student's life. When trying to fully appreciate
the aims and aspirations of a liberal arts education, it is important to keep in mind that the genesis of such an endeavor
began with the Greeks who emphasized that liberty was
synonymous with leisure. In the ancient world, slaves did
the manual labor. Free men possessed leisure and thus asked
the question, "To what end should this leisure be used?" To
the modern student, speaking of leisure as an opportunity
to engage in enigmatic texts and difficult readings is to be
speaking with an antiquarian tongue. Nowadays, leisure is
an occasion for self-indulgence, not self-betterment, a time
to be fruitless without remorse. I know that students feel the
emptiness of this habit. They must. Every year a handful

of students asks me to compile a reading list for them, not because they will ever be tested on these books, but because they understand that there is something basic and essential about certain books and authors. I give them a rudimentary list containing a hodgepodge of novels, works of philosophy and essays.

I shouldn't project an image of my college years as a quasi-monastical period of deep study in which leisure was only used for intellectual pursuits. During those four years there was an interesting duality for me between the wonder and majesty of the classroom versus the licentiousness of the social life on campus. W&L is not just a prestigious liberal arts college, but it is also one of the most die-hard Greek colleges in the country. The popular sentiment was "work hard, play hard." Well over eighty percent of the men are in fraternities and a large portion of the female students are Greek as well. We rank notoriously high in *The Princeton Review*'s rankings of hard liquor and beer consumption. I remember with utter clarity the pointed disappointment The Axe expressed when he began to hear about all the shenanigans synonymous with Greek life. And while he didn't literally shed tears about the hazing and the drinking, I knew he had to be a little disconcerted about the apparent schism between the honorability of students in the classroom and the celebratory embrace of the decadent in their social lives. It is one thing to write a paper demonstrating mastery of a text, but it is quite another to live a life according to these same high-minded principles. What bothered him, I'm sure, is the same thing that always bothers me when I chaperone my school's spring prom. One teaches in the hopes of spawning growth. I know I do. But to learn of the Janus-like quality of our students is to recede to the depths of bitter disappointment. Our students look at us and our classes with one face but encounter the world with quite another, thus defeating

one of the highest aims of the liberal arts which is to synthe-
size the two.

This isn't to say I was a paragon of virtue all the time.
While I rarely drank because of a horrid history of alcohol-
ism in my family, I did join a fraternity. I'll be frank. We
weren't exactly the cool kids on the W&L campus. Our poor
showing at intramurals and the scant attendance by soror-
ity girls at our parties clearly demonstrated this unfortunate
privation of popularity in our social lives. We were the guys
who wouldn't have been Greek on any other campus in
America. We were, at best, fraternal ventriloquists. We wore
the t-shirts, threw the parties, lived in the house. But none
of us really wanted to be hazed. We didn't walk the walk. In
fact, when I went back to attend my five-year reunion the
current fraternity members had taken down the composite
pictures from our era because our tragically unhip status was
a source of embarrassment to them.

I wish I could claim that my fraternity always upheld
the highest ideals of Greek friendship, but it wouldn't be the
truth. Perhaps the best example of this deficiency came my
sophomore year during the house's annual Christmas Party.
For years the fraternity across the street, Kappa Alpha, or
"KA" for short, had given an assignment to their pledges to
steal our Christmas tree, an assignment they were annoyingly successful at completing. After a number of years of
humiliation, we decided to finally make our stand.

We put the tree in the basement of the house, right next
to the back door. For a week or so before the party we uri-
nated into large plastic trash cans in the bathroom that were
conveniently located two floors above the back door. We
also took the liberty of loading enormous squirt guns with
urine. When the time came for them to invade our house,
we mounted a very original defense. As they attempted to
open the back door we emptied the urine-filled trash cans

from the bathroom two floors above. Strategically placed sharp shooters began unloading the squirt guns on the KA pledges. What sticks out in my mind twelve years later is watching a young man getting squirted on his chest and suddenly yelling out in a thick Southern accent, "Oh my GAWD, is that piss on my shirt?"

I don't remember if they got the tree that year, but I do remember some of the brothers being disciplined by a committee on campus. (Being a passive observer has its advantages). I do not write with any authority about the spirit of friendship that was or was not present in other houses. I am sure each of the sixteen houses that were present at the time believed in their own fraternal élan. I freely admit we didn't have the best parties on campus and we certainly weren't a rowdy bunch by comparison. But when I reflect on the many blessings I have received in my life, few rank higher than the extraordinary group of young men I befriended during my four years in this fraternity. And it is in their company that I truly began to understand a different dimension of what it means to become an educated human being. The former president of Washington & Lee University, John Wilson, once noted that education is nothing but an extended conversation among people with interesting minds. And because of my association with these young men, some of whom I still consider to be my best friends in the entire world, I came to appreciate what it means to share in the visions and viewpoints of others.

The magic of classroom dialectics and inspirational lectures carry significant weight in the mind of a student, but a late night discussion among a group of friends as they stand outside their fraternity rooms kindles a kind of intimacy of the spirit that can only be present for a few fleeting moments of life. I close my eyes and can still see the four or five of us holding court on the upstairs landing of our fraternity house during our senior years. I remember thinking at the time that any screenwriter or playwright would have fertile ground if he were to eavesdrop on our eccentric conversations. They ran the gamut from the ridiculous to the profound. But in those conversations that had no direction or inner-logic to them, I discovered that genuine friendships are those that allow you to voice your fears and frailties, your quirks and prejudices. Our fraternity house was the furthest from the campus and I can recall the long walk to campus everyday. I remember, in particular, tutoring my friend on the philosophy readings he never completed. (He ended up getting a higher grade in the class). I remember sitting at a long table at the downtown pub, The Palms, and screaming at the top of my lungs that, because of the geographic distance between us, my girlfriend in California was my Penelope and I was her Odysseus. I remember sitting atop a giant rock that was protruding in the middle of Goshen Pass, a beautiful passage of the Maury River with rock-laden sides and lush plant life, explaining to one of my best friends how nervous and anxious I felt about my impending college graduation.

By the time I reached my senior year, my level of confusion about where I wanted to go and what I wanted to do with my life had reached a delirious pitch. For all the love and appreciation I had for The Axe, his brand of education didn't empower me to answer the one question I seemed to think about the most: what was I going to do next year? In some ways, my love of learning, of books and ideas, had muddied my view of what I was to become. There were now two autonomous elements to my being. Like a delicate stalemate on the verge of calamity, these two sides were about to be at war with one another. The first part was the residue of my former self, of the young man who harbored great ambitions for his life, the one who merely wanted to connect the next dot and continue on the trajectory established long ago. But there was a separate and distinct part of me that was afraid of putting down the books and ignoring the questions. I couldn't imagine a life where my toils and efforts were wholly divorced from the brand of living that enchanted me for the past three-and-a-half years. My problem, of course, was that I conceived of these two world-views as distinct and mutually exclusive.

Two events intervened that quickly fused them together: a book and a death.

During the fall of my senior year, I took a class entitled "Philosophy of Literature." This class was located in my favorite room on the W&L campus, a room we called "The Moon Room" because there was a giant wall-size picture of the Earth as it appears from the surface of the moon. I remember sitting through a laborious three-hour seminar on Kierkegaard every Monday afternoon during the fall of my sophomore year while staring at this picture for long stretches of time. How could I not transport myself to some other-worldly location while discussing a book that described itself as "A Mimical-Pathetical-Dialectical Compilation." I loved the class and have grown fonder of Kierkegaard as I age, but even now I can't imagine what in the hell that phrase means. No wonder I spent long periods gazing at the topography of the Earth from the surface of the moon.

By my senior year I learned that you had to arrive early to class to get a chair that faced the picture. It seems I wasn't the only one who enjoyed the celestial staring. One of the first books we were assigned was Leo Tolstoy's *The Death of Ivan Ilyich*. The professor gave us few introductory comments about the book. He only asked that we read it in one sitting, as it is not a novel but a novella. He remarked that great books speak to us differently in our twenties than in our thirties and forties and so on. I shrugged and assumed I would only read the book once.

That evening I sat down to read the novella. During my senior year I lived on the top floor of the fraternity house. Our fraternity had dwindled in numbers so I lived in a double by myself. It was the closest thing I ever had to a bachelor pad. The bed was vaulted to make space for an old couch that had been passed down through the fraternal generations. I even had a television and a VCR—luxury accommodations by collegiate standards. It was a corner room with two windows. One window looked out at the mountains and the other provided a view of a tall tree that grew alongside the fraternity house. In the corner I had created a reading nook equipped with a rocking chair and a lamp to my side.

I turned off all the lights except for the lamp. It was nine or ten o'clock in the evening and it was starting to storm outside. As I made my way through the book, the wind brushed the tree against the house, resulting in an unnerving mimicry reminiscent of nails on a chalkboard. Thunder shook the house. But no matter what happened outside, I was slowly, page by page, coming under the transcendent spell of Tolstoy for the first time.

I cannot emphasize enough the immediate effect this work had on me. Lightning struck both outside and inside that evening. I saw in Tolstoy's protagonist a life that was consistent with my own "ideal" trajectory. If I continued to connect the dots in the fashion I had always imagined for myself, then my fate would surely mirror that of Ivan Ilyich. Ivan Ilyich did what most people do: he readily acquiesced to conventional wisdom. He accepted the simple answers to the most important of questions. And while the book is a profound study of what it means to die, it ultimately triumphs on a deeper level by demonstrating how we should live. More accurately, it depicts the most horrifying of existential conundrums: to suddenly understand the flaws of one's life without the power or time to remedy them. It took a long, painful death to teach Ivan that he had lived "falsely," that by embracing a life that was both passionless and provincial he missed out on the essential ingredients of a meaningful life. Ivan chose a career and a judgeship that gave him power and prestige but no transcendent purpose. He lived through a disillusioned marriage that had long ago grown cold and stale. He kept his children at a distance. As he lies writhing in pain with nothing to occupy him but the torture of his memories, he begins to understand that true agony doesn't emanate from the body.

As Tolstoy writes towards the end of the novella:

> "It occurred to him that what had seemed utterly inconceivable before – that he had not lived the kind of life he should have— might in fact be true. It occurred to him that those scarcely perceptible impulses of his to protect what people of high rank considered good, vague impulses which he had always suppressed, might have been precisely what mattered, and all the rest had not been the real thing. His official duties, his manner of life, his family, the values adhered to by people in society and in his profession—all these might not have been the real thing. He tried to come up with a defense of these things and suddenly became aware of the insubstantiality of them all. And there was nothing left to defend."

I closed the book with tears in my eyes. In my mind's eye I was transported to a distant time, a distant place, to a non-specific office doing heaven-knows-what. It was the ghost of Christmas future without the Christmas. I imagined myself wearing a fancy suit and sitting in a cubicle somewhere, doing what important people do. As I conjured this image of my future self, I knew that it was within my grasp. I knew that I could be everything I once longed for. The problem was that I also knew that it was now a hollow aspiration, barren of potentiality for the man I now wanted to become.

Ten years and hundreds of books later, I am still enthralled when reading *The Death of Ivan Ilyich*. Perhaps the thrill is knowing that it was a decisive event in my life. It reminds me of Kafka's saying that, "A book must be an ice-axe to break the seas frozen inside our soul." I remember thinking at the time that this was a paper I was excited to write. This was the third class I had taken with this professor, a man surely not at the end of his career but one with more days behind him than in front of him. I had taken two of the most difficult courses in the philosophy department with him, one on Soren Kierkegaard and the other on Ludwig Wittgenstein. Philosophy of Literature was pedestrian by comparison. I had never written a paper for his class that received anything lower than an "A-." But on the paper I wrote about Ivan Ilyich, I received a "B" with the comment that it was fine but it didn't say anything new or particularly interesting about the work. I wanted to defend myself: sure, maybe I didn't say anything new in the annals of human thought. But it was a dashing realization for me: we do more than simply live life. We think about life and thus can change the nature of who and what we are. We are not animals because we are not slaves to our instinct. We can rise above it. We can shape and form it through the use of our mental and spiritual faculties. And while man is not wholly malleable, he operates in an arena of existence that is broader and richer than I had ever imagined. If only Ivan had realized his indeterminate nature sooner, perhaps the torment of his deathbed could have been assuaged by the power of self-knowledge.

I was determined not to suffer a similar fate.

Despite the rapture of this discovery, I still had a problem. All I knew was that I didn't want to work in an office, wearing a suit, ignoring my love of the subjects I was currently studying. This is much different than a definitive answer to what I was going to do with my life. Unfortunately, that definitive answer came in the most tragic of packages.

During Thanksgiving Break of my senior year, my older sister, Sara, suddenly passed away at the age of thirty-four. Sara was my closest sibling—the one who begged my parents to bring my crib into her room, the one who took me on my first outing to the park when I was just two years old, the one who always made me feel I was not alone even though I was the last of five children with a generation between us. She had been battling a variety of ailments ranging from obesity to fibromyalgia and lupus. She sent her young daughter off to school one morning and decided to go back to bed. She never woke up again. Her husband came home later that afternoon. Sara looked like she always looked while sleeping; her right arm safely nestled above her head.

Her heart had simply stopped beating.

This is not the place to chronicle the nuances of every heart-breaking memory between the moment my brother told me she had died to the moment I boarded a plane for Virginia five days later to take my final exams. But there was a constancy beyond grief that stands out about that particular week of my life. I waited for the moment of unbridled, uncontrollable grief to flow over me. I sought and prayed for the tears. I thought I would break down the first time I saw my parents after hearing the news. I thought I would weep at the viewing. I assumed I would lose my composure during her funeral. I remember being summoned to my childhood bedroom by my parents. My remaining brothers and sisters and her husband were all there. We were told to think about her obituary. We all sat there, silent and motionless, waiting for the Muse to assuage our sadness. And still, I was numb.

Sara had been sick for quite some time and none of us expected her to make it to her fifties. But to die this young, with a daughter in the fourth grade, with so much left to do in life, was not a reality I was prepared to confront. My mother was just a few years from retirement when Sara died. She and Sara had detailed plans about what they were going to do together once she retired. But the daily morning walks and volunteer activities never came to pass. Instead, my mother and father slowly had to accept the reality of her eternal absence. My mother was never the same after Sara's death; I'm still not sure if my mother's problem was psychological or existential.

For years, I assumed my unexpected strength during that week was simply a byproduct of denial, a function of my weak brain not being able to process the truth of a new and harsh reality suddenly being thrust upon it. Now that a decade has passed, however, I know that something very different, almost miraculous, was the cause of my stoicism. I knew that Sara's death was not just a chance for me to question my life, but to extrapolate from the tragedy of her death. Sara's death prompted the questions I had been avoiding since my senior year began: what kind of a man did I truly want to be? What was the highest good in my own life? If the measure of a man is somehow connected to the intimacy he facilitates between what he thinks and how he acts, then what kind of a future did I want for myself? If I were in a coffin with my loved ones looking at me, what is it I hope they would say about the life I had lived?

If there was anything I learned in my four years at W&L it is that convictions are rarely convenient. The convictions that matter are the ones that have often been held in doubt, the ones that force us to sometimes be unpopular or turn our backs on an object of temptation. I had finally come to embrace the conviction that I wanted to be the type of man who would return to his family when they needed him most. I wanted to be the type of man who would watch over his young niece and see her through to college since she no longer had a mother. I wanted to be the type of man that shared the splendors of education with others because I knew—through tragedy and grace—the essential ingredient it should play in everyone's life.

I flew back to Virginia after Thanksgiving weekend with my sister's funeral fresh in my mind and the words of Ivan Ilyich still echoing in my head. Oddly enough, I no longer found myself questioning my next step in life. I knew where I was going and what I was doing.

I would like to think that in the ten years since I last spoke with Sara that I have become the kind of man she would be proud to call her brother. She never saw one of my classes, never made it to my wedding or held any of my children in her arms. In many ways, if she were alive today, this memoir would not be written—Sara would surely have been the soundboard against which I bashed my many classroom agonies and elations. But what Sara's death crystallized for me is that there is no time to ignore the truths of one's conscience. I knew that, to many, coming home after college would have all the appearances of failure, of a young man who left brimming with ambition and wanderlust only to return to the tedium of the family profession.

But those voices had to be ignored. If there was one

thing a liberal arts education taught me, it was that the only
voice that matters when making life and death decisions
is your own. I had worked very hard for four years trying
to find and beautify that voice—challenging it, cultivating
it, improving it through the magic of the classroom; for if
education attempts to realize the Socratic ideal of self-knowledge, then I had, at last, graduated with high honors.

I knew I needed the classroom. I needed my friends
and my family. I needed to live a life that aspired to more
than mere possession.

I needed to return home.

CHAPTER II
MY FATHER: MASTER TEACHER

Teaching will always be a matter of life and death for me.

Y ou see, my parents met during a teacher-parent conference. My father was my older brother's junior high
school teacher. My mother was a single widow in
the midst of raising four children. Within two years of that
meeting, they were married, my father adopted my four
future siblings and, most importantly, I had been conceived.
(Timed just right for a summer vacation birth, I might add).
My very existence is the product of a love that sprouted in
a classroom. Whatever concupiscence was present in the
classroom that winter day eventually translated into my
birth. I cannot help but feel as I look back on my life—its
beginning and its present state—that the power of the classroom has always been with me and in me. Being raised by
two teachers who met in a classroom and produced a child
who fell in love with the exchange of ideas is not a particu-

larly surprising tale to tell.

To really understand my particular burden, however, it is not necessary to observe my father's classroom or recollect the romance between my parents. No, my burden is best understood by framing it around my earliest memory.

It revolves around my father and the family dog.

When I was four years old I mysteriously stumbled upon my older brother, Howard, digging a massive hole in the backyard while uncontrollably weeping. I don't remember what I asked him or how I phrased my question. But he was having none of it. He didn't want to talk. He just wanted to dig. He just wanted to weep. I later came to understand that there is a magical symbiosis in human life, between tears and manual labor: weeping in silent isolation is undeniably pathetic, yet tears in the midst of mindful labor are somehow heroic. It's a Greek and enigmatic sentiment, yes, and my brother could stomach the tears but not the lethargy that accompanies them.

I ran back into the house. I remember it was hot, even for the San Joaquin Valley of California. But before opening the backdoor, I looked back at my older brother one more time. He was still digging but suddenly stood up, leaned on the shovel for just a second, and delicately wiped away the moisture that had collected on the plateau of his right cheek. Fluid leapt from his red cheeks and into the shallow ditch; before the fluid hit the ground, he was digging anew. I will never know how much of the fluid was sweat and how much was tears, but it was of no consequence. The soil was now consecrated. My brother was not digging a large hole for a plant or a tree, but a shallow grave for the body of the family dog: Barney.

What I suddenly understood was that the family dog—a half Beagle, half Basset Hound that resulted in the affectionately created neologism 'Barney Boogle'—was dead and that my pang of sadness was not exclusively mine. It also belonged to my two older brothers—the one digging the grave and my other brother, Will, who was in transit from the veterinarian's office with the dog's body in his possession. Everyone claimed that Barney was Will's dog, but what I knew at the age of four was that Barney slept in my bed every evening. Some four-year olds clutch to dolls or stuffed animals. I had Barney Boogle when I went to bed. I remember Barney slowly trudging up the nineteen stairs to my bedroom. Barney would patiently sit at the foot of my bed as my parents followed the nightly routine. First they would read me a story and then they would pick me up and allow me to kiss all the Disney character posters adorning my bedroom.

Not long after Barney's death Will left for the Army and I was left alone in a big, Victorian house with no siblings and a cadre of empty rooms. These rooms would be reoccupied intermittently by siblings who couldn't make up their minds about the challenges of early adulthood. Perhaps the premature liberation of adulthood made them clutch to the fixtures of a childhood they had long resisted in their earlier teenage years. But for the most part, I was left to fend for myself in a giant house with no siblings and, more tragically, no Barney Boogle.

In these years between pets I never felt ignored; after all, my parents still loved parenting and still had a weighty project on their hands with me. I never felt abandoned; joining the army or leaving for college or moving into an apartment with friends seemed like natural paths for all of my much-older siblings. But I did feel lonely. And I knew there was but a single remedy.

I made a request to my father for a new dog, which yielded a six-year process that was Homeric in scope and epic in length. I wanted a dog that was as similar to Barney as possible so we settled on a pure blooded Bassett Hound.

Every Saturday morning after my mother and I had taken our Saturday bike ride to Mc Donald's, we would purchase a newspaper and search the classifieds for Basset Hounds as we consumed our sausage McMuffins and hash browns. Every few months my hopes for a new dog were rekindled as we found a Bassett Hound for sale.

Invariably this hope met the same fruitless end: my mother would call for an appointment, we would visit a house or a kennel or a ranch, I would fall in love with one of the puppies, and my father would curtly say thank you and leave without purchasing a dog for me. I remember on one particular occasion crying in the backseat with my mother coming to my defense.

"I don't see why we just can't get him a dog, Larry. We're not entering the pup in a dog show for God's sake!"

Yet my father was steadfast in his pursuit of canine excellence. My mother and I were both making the same assumption about my father. He spent much of his twenties on the dog show circuit, breeding dogs, and acquiring an encyclopedic mind about the particulars of canine perfection. He knew the difference between a real Basset Hound and one that was watered down by the taint of imperfection. Some people won't drink cheap wine or wear plastic sunglasses. Well, my father wasn't going to give his youngest child a mutt for a childhood dog.

After years of tears, turmoil, and torrents of confusion, we hopelessly found another advertisement in the paper—by now I was in fifth grade and, on this issue, deeply in despair. I remember little about the particular outing except that as I picked up the tiny hound and breathed in the familiar puppy aroma, my father inexplicably asked the question I never thought I would hear: "How much should I write the check for?"

I can safely assume that jubilation immediately flooded the inner-cavern of my young soul. Yet to be honest, there is only one other moment from that day that occasionally flickers in my mind's eye after all of these years. It is the moment that simultaneously explains so much of my father that is both grand and taxing. As soon as we got in the car with the Basset safely sitting on my lap, my father looked around to the backseat with a curious look splashed across his face. It wasn't exactly a visage of happiness. It wasn't filial pride, either. In fact, his expression had nothing to do with me: it was the look of a man who knew he was right all along. My tears and my mother's pleas to let me have an inferior dog had tempted him. But he persisted. To my father, buying a dog was like anything else in life: that which is meaningful should never be easy. The things that are easy, that spring from nature or from caprice, are illusionary accomplishments rooted as much in chance as excellence. Buying the first dog would have been easy. It would have felt good in the moment. But it wouldn't have been the right dog, the dog my father always had faith was out there waiting for me, the dog who was my one constant companion throughout childhood.

This defining conviction of my father's—that illusionary accomplishments are for other people, but not for him or his son—has always served him well. As a child, he had a home, even if it wasn't much of one. The Kern River slices through our hometown, Bakersfield, California. The metaphor of living across the railroad tracks can aptly apply to my father—except it wasn't a railroad he lived across, it was a river. On the other side of the Kern is a suburb of sorts, a place called Oildale, or as my father-in-law sarcastically calls it, "God's Country." Poor white folks, especially those who make their livings with their backs and trucks, populate the dusty suburb of Oildale. My grandfather was not cut from the same

cloth as my father. He struggled with the bottle for as long as
my father could remember him. My grandparents had been
married for over a decade before they conceived my father.
My father never full elaborated on the reproductive tribula-
tions of his parents. Needless to say, the doctors told them
they would never bear any children of their own. Within a
year of the doctor's verdict, my father was born.

 I never knew either of my grandparents, but from what
I can gather, my father never really understood his own
father. My grandfather worked at a laundry mat. His job
was to collect and manage the tokens that were used in the
laundry machines and driers. Not exactly a glamorous job.
But they were never homeless or in need of government assistance. They moved around quite a bit in search of cheap
housing. By the time my father reached high school, they
were living in a dilapidated shack in the middle of Oildale.
My father showed it to me once. I remember waiting for
some additional commentary from him but all he did was
point and tell me that's where he spent his high school years.
He was so embarrassed by the place that he never let anyone
visit except for his best friend. But he always had a sense
that he could do better. He believed the past was only a prologue, never a predictor of what was to come. He marched
in the band and became drum major. He read veraciously,
keenly interested in World War II and Asian histories. He
joined the military for two years when he graduated from
high school. This experience might not be the equivalent of
summers in Europe or an education from Phillips Exeter or
Groton, but it was enough to give him an understanding of a
richer life than what he had been given. When he returned
from military service in Korea, he worked at a jewelry store
and as a repo man. Selling cheap diamonds and dodging
dogs was never going to be enough to satisfy him so he put
himself through the local college while helping his parents

on the side. It is the same American tale that has been lived and told countless times.

By the age of twenty-seven he was teaching junior high English. The school, Emerson Junior High, was located in the middle of one of the roughest neighborhoods in Bakersfield. (I had the vast misfortune of attending the place for two years and still believe they are the worst two years of my life though I'm not sure if it was the place or prepubescent angst). There was a healthy amount of busing from middle class neighborhoods and my father quickly got assigned the upper-level students. It didn't matter if it was the spelling bee or a speech competition; my father worked, pushed, and sometimes even cajoled his students into every competition imaginable. He did so well and won so often that one of the trustees of the Bakersfield City School District once approached him at a meeting and hastily inquired, "Do you always have to win everything?"

Feeling somewhat vexed and underappreciated, my father made his exodus from junior high in 1984 and decided to try his hand at high school teaching and coaching the speech and debate team. Five years later, when I was twelve years old, my father's speech and debate team won the California State Championship. This had been my father's grandest ambition for the better part of a decade. He was relentless in pursuing it. Until the sixth grade, the only nightly entertainment I ever knew didn't come from the television, but from high school students who were at our house practicing their speeches. There were humorous and dramatic presentations, classical oratories, truncated debates modeled after Abraham Lincoln and Stephen Douglas. It was then that I developed a strong appreciation for the spoken word, of its potential power and spellbinding allure.

Words are not merely vehicles of cold mental images, but can be catalysts of transcendent inspiration. To ascend to such rhetorical heights is to commit to hours and hours of composition, memorization, and eventual execution. There were so many students coming in and out of our home on a nightly basis that our neighbors began to suspect my parents were drug dealers. My father and his speech team spent over twenty seven weekends away during the 1987-1988 school year, traveling up and down the state of California competing in tournaments. He would get so nervous before an important tournament that he would vomit. Every Monday morning I awoke to see a different shiny trophy sitting on our breakfast room table. His efforts had not been in vain. His commitment and his zest for excellence bore abundant fruit.

In all the years that he coached the speech and debate team, he only took me to one speech tournament to USC. Most of the team stayed back that weekend for the Winter Formal so he chaperoned just a handful of students. The awards ceremony was held on the top floor of one of the buildings on campus. A dozen or so high school students along with some parents piled into an elevator that promptly ascended to the correct floor and refused to open. I was only in the fifth grade and handling it pretty well until one of the parents said, "I don't think we're getting any air in here. This could be bad." I heard my mother and father on the other side of the elevator door, but it wasn't enough to assuage my fear. My tears were plentiful and loud. Within an hour we were out of the elevator and my father never took me to another speech tournament. I can't say I blame him.

It would be simple to illustrate his excellence by listing his awards and achievements, but a better demonstration of his standing as a quasi-legend in the Bakersfield teaching community would be to explain his relationship with former students. Before I became a teacher I always assumed that all former students treated their former teachers the way they treated my father. But the truth of the matter is that I have never seen a teacher held in higher esteem, more adulated, more loved in the long-run of life as my father. His classes were not the stuff of high theatre or abundant witticisms. He was always tough and always fair. He clearly knew his stuff. But the abundant love former students feel for my father stems from the fact that there was something mysteriously reassuring and patriarchic about his innocuous rigidity— his classroom emanated the glow of stern compassion. My father has been retired for six years and still there is not a Christmas Vacation that passes without a student from his past randomly knocking on his door to say hello. He was invited to more weddings than any man I have ever known who was not a head of state.

At first, I didn't understand why so many of his former students felt the compunction to tell him their life's story. Didn't they understand that they should move on with their lives, that there is something strangely pathetic about adults in their 30's and 40's still seeking the guidance and company of their high school English teacher? Despite the decades that have passed since last being in his classroom, they seek him out because he is still their teacher. And just as any child constantly clamors for the approval of a parent, these students still feel the gravity of my father's presence in their lives. They often return because they want him to know that they are still connected to him, that the respite since being his student has done nothing to cool the flames of their admiration for him.

The class that he taught for twenty years was a survey course of different literary genres. In the fall the class read short stories and poetry. In the spring they studied the history of the English language and read *Julius Caesar* and *Inherit The Wind*. In his prime, my father's classroom was peripatetic *par excellence*. He walked up and down the aisles, randomly quizzed the students, and cultivated a pervading sense that no one was ever safe in his classroom. His class was tailor-made to fit his personality and intellectual strengths. He took great pains every fall to create a classroom aesthetic that complimented the seriousness of his task. I remember spending the waning weeks of summer in his hot classroom putting up new posters, fresh wallpaper, and fancy border. He possessed the biggest classroom on campus and the enormity of the room mirrored the tallness of the task he faced. He wanted his students to walk into his class the first day and immediately perceive that this was not a place of dittos and movies. This was a place where the mind was cherished, where indifference dies, where thinking new thoughts wouldn't be so new.

While he was serious and stern, he was not without his teaching quirks. I have heard stories that in the 1970's he was known around campus as the teacher that wore flaming red pants. He is still a snappy dresser, but definitely more mainstream. Sometime in the late 1990's he found some white socks for sale at an outlet store. He was very proud of them and decided to show them off to his students. They were greatly amused by the fact that these socks were FUBU socks —"For Us By Us"— a brand of clothing that the students told him was intended for African-Americans, not elderly white high school teachers. His most annoying teaching quirk centered on his perennial need to ostentatiously demonstrate oddball pronunciations. He doesn't just use odd pronunciations himself, but insists on correcting others as frequently as humanly possible. His favorites include "Van Gogh" and "forte." To listen to my father, Van Gogh doesn't end with the sound of a long "o," but a "th." Forte doesn't end with a long "a," but is pronounced like a military "fort." The kids just look at him blankly, wondering what it would sound like if they used my father's pronunciation when telling their math teacher, "Math just isn't my forte."

Teachers of my father's quality and ilk are becoming tragically passé. As I look at modern education I am at once saddened and relieved by my father's exit from the classroom; sad because he no longer enriches lives in the way he used to. Relieved because the curricular program my father created, the one that won him the love and accolades of thousands of students, could no longer exist in a modern American classroom. I honestly don't know what he would do in an era of pacing guides, benchmarks, common formative assessments, summative assessments, professional learning communities, state tests, and national tests, just to name a few. This panoply of curricular guidelines is tantamount to death for teachers like my father. How would he respond to cell phones going off, the omniscience of headphones in ears, and students using the powers of modern technology to cheat in the most sophisticated of ways. How would he respond to being rated by students on Internet websites? This is a man who never enjoyed criticism, especially of the public variety and from fourteen year olds.

There is no denying that my father made extraordinary strides in a single lifetime. There is a lot to be proud of and he is a very proud man. But being proud is not the same thing as being satisfied. And while he is happy to have been a high school teacher for thirty years, he often feels the melancholy tug of dissatisfaction. There is an unspoken but palpable sentiment within him that he could have done more, could have been more, could have been someone in a position to make defining decisions for his community and country. These are just raw, inchoate feelings of unrequited ambitions, nothing more. He never fills in the contours of his discontent with the coloring of a specific job or career. But his impeccable logic and love of oratory would have made him a candidate for excellence in law. His eclectic mind and love of young people would have paved the way for a memorable career in the academic world of colleges and universities. He could have gone anywhere and done anything if his family situation had just been a little bit different. He could have attended a more prestigious university and graduated sooner than twenty-seven. But his opportunities were sparse and his parents needed him. And no matter what anybody says, ambition tends to be a virtue fueled by self-love. The nobility of his choice to stay in his hometown, attend the local college and help his parents exacted a price. There was very little self-love in it. I don't think he knows how much I admire him for this decision. But I sometimes wonder if he would make the same series of decisions if he had it to do all over.

For my sake, I certainly hope so.

I wish I could tell you that my father sat down with me at the breakfast room table every evening to dutifully assist me on my homework. He did. But this wasn't a typical situation. He was motivated by more than simple duty. His dissatisfaction reared its head. The routine of homework is well-known to every parent: the child does the homework, gets help from a parent when needed, and then tries his/her best when the time for the test arrives. But I remember understanding, even as a six year old in the first grade, that there was a certain way to approach your tasks. Trying your best isn't good enough. Ambition rocks the cradle of excellence. I wouldn't have stated it in such a way in the first grade, but my father had a masterful way of instilling habits without ever saying a word. Aristotle and my father had similar views on virtue. Virtue, said Aristotle, is an extension of habit, not knowledge. The role of the parent is to facilitate good habits, i.e. virtues. By the time a child matures, their virtue becomes second nature. I don't think my father had any idea how much he succeeded.

It all started in the first grade when I was expected to learn how to read.

Every week my first grade teacher gave us ten or so words to learn how to spell with a thematic element attached to each list. One list may have centered on sports so we learned to spell ball, run, catch, jump. One list may have centered on shapes so we learned circle, square, and triangle. We took our spelling test every Thursday morning. My teacher simply passed out a blank sheet of paper and said the words slowly, one by one. This was the first time in my life I learned what it meant to be nervous, to fear failure with an invective pang in my chest that still echoes twenty-five years later. My father quickly set a goal that I wouldn't miss any words the entire year. Perfection was his aim, hours at the dining room table were his method. I was doing fine until the theme of the week was food. I quickly mastered the spelling of ketchup and relish, but no matter how many times my father quizzed me, I couldn't figure out the spelling of mayonnaise. Even today, just this moment, I rely on spell check. As a six year old I just couldn't remember the double "n." (And just for the record, looking back on it with thirty-two year old eyes, I still consider it to be a ridiculously difficult spelling word for a first grader)! I remember my father being amused by the mayonnaise spectacle until Wednesday evening. I think he was starting to question if my streak was about to end. The moment came early Thursday morning and it was, of course, the last word she asked us to spell. I closed my eyes and tried to see the word. Even then it was apparent I didn't possess a photographic memory. I saw nothing but black. All I could think about was the double "n." However, when I got to the end of the word I forgot the "e." Just as my teacher was about to pick up my paper—her hand might have even been on it for all I remember—I saw my mistake and quickly jotted down the missing "e." She looked at me for a moment and continued down the aisle.

I think my life and world-view would be considerably different today had I misspelled a single word that year, maybe had I left off an "n" or "e." But I didn't. I met my father's challenge and finished the year with the perfection he had asked of me. And although I couldn't articulate it at six years of age, I already understood my father's favorite truth: greatness is not a chance; it is a choice. Excellence doesn't happen on accident. Grand achievement in any venue—a classroom, a boardroom, a playing field—is a consequence of diligent commitment. My father's commitment to finding the right dog or vicariously willing me to spelling perfection implicitly taught me about what's not only possible, but expected. This is the same man who prominently displayed a sign in his classroom for twenty years that said, "You show me a good loser and I'll show you a loser." In other words, this is not a romantic laborer. There is no ecclesiastic glory to putting one's nose to the grindstone. One does not find love or God or anything else in the throws of dedication. My father believed in diligence for no other reason than it worked. There is little erudition behind it.

The residue of his keen understanding about excellence is that it unintentionally provoked in me a life fraught with classroom fear. He never wanted me to react this way to his lofty expectations. Still, henceforth, excellence was no longer reached with the celebratory embrace of accomplishment, but with a deep sigh of relief. I knew early on that to brush up against mediocrity is the full expression of wastefulness. For the first few years of my academic life, I dreaded the school year. I walked to school with butterflies in my stomach. I didn't eat breakfast on the days I knew we would be grading work in class. Every ninth Friday the teacher would pass out quarter grades. I remember my third grade teacher had them sitting on the edge of her desk the entire day, hauntingly close to my own desk. I stared at the pile hour after hour until the last ten minutes of the day. In retrospect, I wonder if she would have given me a sneak peak during recess had I voiced my anxiety.

I remember crying on the way home from school one day because I received a poor grade in math. I wasn't afraid of my father's hand or his words, just his face of disappointment. As I walked up to the crossing guard I had tears in my eyes. The crossing guard, Morris, told me to look up into one of the trees overhead. An egg had fallen from a nest earlier in the day and he explained that the birds had been acting funny ever since. Twenty-five years later and I still have no idea what Morris was trying to tell me. Morris is long gone and I still feel the mighty weight of a father's expectations. I eat breakfast every morning and don't receive report cards, and yet I still feel slivers of nerves every day of my professional life. Sometimes they are close and raw, sometimes distant and minor. I think of the lesson I am about to present to my classes and a small shot of adrenaline shoots somewhere into my body. There is still fear, still an aching not to disappoint the gods of greatness. I am afraid I won't explain the material well enough, afraid I'll bore the students, afraid my students will meet my lesson with indifferent shrugs and blank gazes. But most of all, I am afraid I won't be able to bridge the gap between the vivacity I feel for the material and the external drabness of the classroom. I wish I could be one of those teachers who simply tries his best, presents the material clearly, grades fairly, treats the students respectfully and hopes for good things. I know an army of teachers who go home and don't think about their classroom until the next morning. I know teachers who leave their rooms in May and ignore the failures of the previous year. Yet this is an empty aspiration for me, barren of any hope of realization. The truth is that I am the same little boy with nerves made raw by every misspelled word or poor math grade. The only difference is that now I am a grown man who feels the blow of failure with each disinterested student.

My father's disappointments and regrets, his unrealized ambitions, and lastly, his vast overestimation of my talents and intellect, yoked together to foist upon me a burden of unspeakable weight. Obviously, this was no esoteric burden. My father didn't lull me to sleep at night with soliloquies of grandeur or stories by Horatio Alger. No, this was a very specific burden that was crafted in the light of his own life. To live vicariously through your children is natural. I already do it with my children when they see fireworks for the first time or experience the wonder of Christmas. But to engineer a blueprint for another life can be more than a little daunting for the person who must execute the plans to perfection. And so, when I was young my father started setting goals for me—sometimes small (perfect spelling scores), sometimes large (admittance to an elite university). When I was in elementary school the most prestigious award for graduating sixth graders was the O.D. Williams Award. When I graduated from junior high I was aiming for the Emerson Faculty Award. Once I got to high school my aspiration was to win a Bank of America Plaque.

I once told my father that being his child would either produce an over-achiever or a suicide case. He laughed because he knew which one he got. The problem he had with teaching—at least with me teaching—is that there are no benchmarks and awards. Lawyers win cases. Doctors heal patients. Academics contribute to a body of scholarly knowledge. But to teach is to be stagnant. As my father once told me, "The first day of a teaching career looks awfully similar to the last day of a teaching career." We can hone our craft. We can perfect our lectures. But at the end of the day we are left with the same empty desks, a lectern and some whiteboards. The objects of our art form are gone, and with it our barometers of success.

It is important to pause and note that none of these honors or accolades from my youth were important in their own right. They were each dots on a mosaic of triumph that was supposed to culminate in a picture of grand achievement. My father's recipe was simple: push me hard, hope I execute all that we have practiced, enjoy the splendors of trophies, certificates, and medals, and hope that the sensation of success becomes addictive. By the time I was in high school my father didn't have to say a word. When I played tennis, I wanted to win. When I played the saxophone, I wanted to be sitting in the first chair. When I competed in a speech or debate tournament first place was always the aspiration. The drive. The ambition. The torment of mediocrity. They had all been mindfully inculcated in me like a composer artfully placing notes where they belong on a sheet of music. The composer could now walk away because the performer knew the notes by heart.

I am not sure if the composer ever knew how the symphony was going to end, however. What I quickly discovered is that it was not supposed to end in the same place where it began. I remember sitting in my fraternity bedroom thinking about how I was going to break the news to my father. How was I going to tell him that I wanted to be a high school teacher? He had just lost his daughter. I didn't want him to feel that he was losing his son, albeit in a very different way. I gave him the most heartfelt monologue of my life. I evoked my dead sister. I told him my fears of losing a rich intellectual life I had grown to love. I even told him that I was going to lose my girlfriend in California if I didn't commit to being closer to her after a four year separation. (I was in Virginia. She was law student in California). He was calm but obvious in his disappointment.

"You don't know how bad it's gotten since you've been gone," he told me. "The kids have changed. They're not the same as you remember. Don't you want to go to grad school or get a JD or something?"

To his credit, this is the only time he ever tried to talk me out of entering the teaching profession. It wasn't a terribly long or adversarial conversation. He could have brought up the thousands of dollars he spent on my education or the hours of transportation to tennis tournaments and debate competitions. He could have assumed the role of a classical apologist, defending his view of what my life should be while simultaneously debunking mine. It must have been difficult for him to remain mute when I came home, received a teaching credential from the local college, and ended up in a classroom six doors down from his. He let me know his disapproval in subtle ways. My teaching credential cost two-thousand dollars. A law degree costs well over one-hundred thousand collars. He offered to help me with a law degree, but not the teaching credential.

For many years I was hurt by his disappointment. Part of my problem was that I wasn't used to it. I lived most of my life in accordance with explicit expectations. My greatest fear in life is failure and to fail the one man I loved the most in the world was more than a little disconcerting. There was but a single question he wanted me to correctly answer: what am I to do with the limited amount of time I have in this life? My father wanted the answer I could never provide. He wanted me to become the modern version of what Homer called *agathos*, the man of honor and glory, the man whose worthiness is confirmed by his high estimation in the eyes of others; in this view, the life that matters it the one that is explicitly remembered. This was the world-view of the Mycenaean Greeks who did not gauge the luster of a man's life by his fidelity to a domestic world of family and community. Achilles rejected a view of life that championed compassion over accomplishment, love over glory. It is the man who strives for the masculine legacies of fame through strength who captures the prize of mass adulation. That is why my father had no preference about the outlet of my success. He simply wanted me to pick a career that would easily give rise to the outward markers of achievement. If ever there was a profession that did exactly the opposite, it is surely teaching. For me to sanctify the banal or give affirmation to the ordinariness of a classroom was a horrific prospect to a father who had spent a lifetime carefully manicuring a successful trajectory for me. What I wanted was nothing exceptional. Empty accolades and ignorant applause was not what I wanted. I wanted what every man can have—a meaningful marriage, loving children, a career that softens the tragedy of lying in a deathbed years in the future. Perhaps it wasn't exceptional. Perhaps I would never have my name in the history books. But that wasn't what I wanted any more. What I wanted was not all that different from the life my father had. But I wanted it for very different reasons.

In a certain sense, my father was a memorable teacher precisely because he did not approach his craft with an ordinary playbook. He, himself, was Achilles in the classroom. His excellence was an extension of his superhuman competitiveness. My father didn't simply challenge his students because it spurred academic growth. He challenged them because he was competing with other schools, other teachers, and yes, even the ever-fleeting notion of pedagogic perfection itself. It's an odd catalyst for classroom excellence. It's like an athlete being motivated by beauty or a writer who writes lyrical works of great profundity, but who is really only motivated by greed. He was an apostle of an ancient world-view, the honor ethic, in which the darker impulses

of one's character can be purified if they are in service of a
higher ideal. Achilles was vainglorious and brooding but
his heroics helped to win the Trojan War. My father's competitiveness, his insecurity, his aversion to criticism, worked
together to ferment a teacher of exceptional quality. Indeed,
it brings to mind one of La Rochefoucauld's most famous
maxims: "What we call virtues are often just a collection
of casual actions and selfish interests which chance or our
own industry manages to arrange [in a certain way]. It is not
always from valor that men are valiant, or from chastity that
women are chaste."

I do understand the root of his bitter disappointment
about my choice. After all, his life story is a shining example
of the progress that can be made in a single lifetime. He had
gone from Oildale to the pinnacle of the teaching profession
in one lifetime. And because my life began from a much
more privileged perch, my potential for growth was infinitely higher. My life was supposed to continue the trajectory started by my father. I was supposed to be a lawyer, an
academic, an elected official or a journalist. Instead, my life
became a "lateral life," a life that merely continued what my
father started but in no way surpassed it. There is a good
chance I won't even equal my father's teaching achievements.
He is a tough act to follow. Still, I wanted to tell him that being a high school teacher with ambition is not oxymoronic.
And while he clearly wanted more for me than what he ever
had, I always felt that my life was plenty privileged and more
than full. Teaching afforded my parents the type of life I
wanted to share with my own family—a type of life where
the mind is treasured and where vacations are plentiful.
Granted, there was little opulence and luxury, but I couldn't
miss something I never had.

A lateral life didn't frighten me just as long as it was
my life. But there was one regret I immediately had before

taking my first step into the classroom. I wasn't sure my father would ever be proud of me the way he was when I was younger. I remember his tears when I opened my acceptance letter to college. I remember him jumping up and down when I captured an important tennis title when I was fourteen years old. He once told my wife that the happiest times of his life occurred when visiting me for W&L's Parent Weekend. He was happy, of course, because he thought I was on the right trajectory. But now these moments of glee were going to be scarce for my father, if not extinct. I knew when making the decision to become a teacher that he would be proud of me as a person, that I would always be loyal to my wife and loving to my children, but the occasions of jubilant paternal pride were going to be rare. There are instances in a young person's life when insecurity must be forsaken in the hopes of something finer, something more honorable than the reflexive desire for parental approval. This was such a moment for me.

And so it came to pass in the fall of 1998, just three months after graduating from college, that I went to work at the very high school I had graduated from just four years earlier. More interestingly, I was now working alongside my father in the same department. It was a large shadow to work beside. Had my father been a relatively normal teacher, teaching average students in an average way, it would have been far easier for me to make a name for myself. But sharing a name with a teaching giant in a relatively self-contained community carries both significant advantages and burdens. His enemies transposed their dislike onto me. It took them many years to figure out that we are immensely different people. My father feeds on conflict and I avoid it at all costs. My father is steady and stern in the classroom. I am a bit flamboyant and forgiving. He is interested in Art History and has eclectic tastes when it comes to literature. I have a

few intellectual interests—politics, philosophy, education—
and rarely stray from them. But most of all, I was working
from a blank canvass. My father was known and respected
by hundreds of families whereas I had to start from scratch.
He always taught GATE (Gifted & Talented Education)
classes and I was teaching mid to low level students my first
two or three years.

This was not the first time our classroom journeys
intersected. When I was a freshman in high school, I had
the uncomfortable honor of being a student in his advanced
English class. There were no other teachers who taught this
advanced English course. I remember my first order of business was trying to figure out what to call him. I had a few
ideas. Mr. Adams? Pop? Dad? Hey You? I finally decided
on "Dad" since everyone in the world knew I was his son—
misplaced and faux formality would have appeared more
than a little odd. The year went smoothly with one minor
hiccup. In the midst of his unit on the history of the English
language, which his students always labeled as the HOTEL
unit, he mentioned the book *Beowulf*. At fourteen I had
never heard of the book so when my best friend sarcastically
said, "Oh, I've read that," I turned to him and said, "Cory,
you're so stupid." Sensing that my snipe was inappropriate,
my father intervened on Cory's behalf.

"Young man, you don't know what stupid is."

I looked him straight in the face while pointing my
index finger at him and bravely said, "Yes, I do."

He said nary a word, walked halfway down the aisle,
picked up my backpack, and threw it like he was participat-
ing in the hammer throw at the Olympics. It dramatically hit
the floor before slamming into the classroom door.

"Get out," he yelled. A few minutes later he came outside and said the most truculent thing I could ever imagine.

"Your mother will take care of this when you get home."

Our overlapping existence played out in humorous ways as well. By teaching at the same high school, I became "Young Adams," to the chagrin of my father who became, of course, "Old Adams." I encouraged the kids to simply call me "Good Looking Adams," but it never stuck for obvious reasons. We even shared students. He taught the advanced English class for freshmen and I eventually taught the advanced World History class for freshmen. The students would meander down the hallway from his classroom to mine, full of stories about me from my childhood that I constantly had to correct. He even passed out an unfortunate picture of me from my college years. It was taken in the middle of the night when three or four of my fraternity brothers and I were having one of those long conversations about nothing. I had taken off my shirt and flexed for the camera for reasons I still cannot remember, or perhaps I just don't want to. Whatever the case, the picture was blown up and made into a poster to the amusement of everyone on campus but me. An interesting young lady once came out of my father's first period class and announced that if she were old enough to be "on the receiving end of a senior discount" she would happily date my dad. Once the nausea abated, I had to admit that it was a funny comment. We even went to lunch together most days.

At one of those lunches he told me about the day I left for college. My mother had volunteered to take me back to Virginia to help set up my dorm room and get me settled in. Sara and my father dropped the two of us off at the airport. Before 9/11 it was still common to walk a loved one to the departing gate and watch as the plane took off. Bakersfield did not have a particularly modern airport. They still used a ramp to enter and exit planes. As I walked up the ramp, I saw my sister and father waving goodbye. My mother and

I waved back and boarded the plane, eager to begin a new
chapter in my life. I remember my departure from the vantage point of the person leaving. My father told me that it
looked very different to him. He and my sister watched the
plane speed down the runway, take off, and quickly turn east.
Within a few seconds the plane disappeared into the clouds
and was out of sight. I didn't know until years later that my
father turned to my sister and sighed, "As fast as that plane
vanished, eighteen years vanished faster."

L ast year my father had the unfortunate task of speaking
at a memorial service in honor of a former student who
had recently committed suicide. This student was one of
my father's all-time favorites, the kind of kid you never want
to grow up so you can keep him in your class forever. I sat
by my father in the pew as he waited for his cue to go to the
front of the church. He turned to me and said in a whisper,
"If you teach long enough, something like this always happens." He eloquently recalled the young man as exceptionally intelligent and funny, peppering his talk with anecdotes
from happier days. Afterwards there was a small dinner
in the dining hall of the church where he saw friends and
former students for the first time in decades. In the midst of
such a tragic gathering, I wondered how many teachers ever
got close enough to their students to merit delivering a eulogy at a service. It is a charge I hope I am never given. Still,
it underlines the level of commitment my father made to his
students. That is why we could never go to the mall when
I was younger. We could rarely venture out in anonymity
without former students approaching my father en masse to
offer their greetings and hellos.

Early one morning, shortly after my father delivered the
eulogy, there was a curious knock on his front door. With

disheveled hair and a bit of disorientation, my father saun-
tered down the stairs and opened the door. A man in his
mid-forties who looked vaguely familiar stood wide-eyed on
his front porch.

"Can I help you?" my father inquired.

The man told my father that his name was "Lance." He
was a student in the first junior high school class my father
ever taught, long ago, in 1973.

"I just came by because I became a father for the first
time this morning. For some reason I wanted you to be one
of the first people to know." My father thanked him and
Lance abruptly hopped down the front porch stairs and continued on his way.

What I have learned from my father, the master teacher,
is that to teach is to intertwine your life with thousands of
others that have experienced the rich spectrum of human
possibilities. Within a month my father had brushed up
against the tragedy of death and the rhapsody of new life, all
because he had been a committed teacher for thirty years. I
wonder what more any of us can ever ask out of life than to
experience this wondrous vitality of human connectedness.
Teaching, if it is done well and with the proper degree of
passion, can and should be a matter of life and death. If it is
done well, it is a calling and a craft.

My father retired five years ago and still he lives by
the academic clock and calendar. He looks at the clock at
10:15 am and immediately knows that we are in the middle
of third period. He glances at the calendar in October and
recalls that this was the part of the year when he taught "The
Necklace" by Guy de Maupassant. On Thursdays he misses
the endless squirming of students on "grammar day," the day
he tormented them with gerund phrases, conjunctions, and
prepositions. You can retire from the classroom, but that
doesn't mean it retires from your immediate consciousness.

For years he had a fantasy about his first day of retirement. He wanted to thunder down the runway on a giant 747 heading for Europe at the exact moment when the bell for first period rang on the first day of school. He had grandiose visions of sitting back in his plane seat and saying, "So Long Suckers!" But instead he missed the classroom more than he could imagine. In the five years since he has retired, he has come back to long-term sub a number of times. He always wants to know the latest gossip and movements on campus. He finally broke down and told me that he retired about two years too early. Retirees often play a game of follow-the-leader. My father didn't want to win the game, but he certainly didn't want to be excluded from it either.

His friends and colleagues were retiring and he didn't want to be the teacher who didn't recognize his time had passed, the one the administrators always hoped would finally figure it out. He saw in himself the boxer who was once great but didn't know when to stop fighting. He loves traveling to Asia and fixing up the house. What's difficult about retirement, he once told me, is that one must forfeit an anchor of his/her identity. So much of his essence was linked to his profession. When it vanished, he couldn't help but experience minor vertigo. For many people there is a great disconnect between what they do and who they are. My wife is an attorney, but if we won the lottery tomorrow she wouldn't lament a sudden loss of identity. My brother is a correctional officer, but he would be the same man if he were an accountant. To my father, it is incidental if he works at a high school or out of his living room. He is a teacher.

I cast no aspersions towards those who teach for a paycheck or a summer vacation. After all, most teachers are practitioners, not poets, of education. Great teachers are born, not made. But for classroom practitioners, there is little elation and rarely any tragedy, only the dull monotony of a classroom that is neither memorable nor warm. My father was not a perfect teacher—he was on the impatient side and had no tolerance for the slightest tincture of philistinism. He resembled Bear Bryant in the classroom. Bryant's words on the first day of practice could easily have been my father's on the first day of school: "Be good or be gone!" In thirty years of teaching he experienced the full gamut of what a teacher can experience. At least the rocks that he has thrown come back to tell him about the waves they've created and the rivulets they've occupied.

In the ten years since I've become a teacher, I would like to think he has made peace with my decision to enter the classroom. The years of sharing both students and a lunch period forged a new bond between us, one that took on a different tenor and tone than my childhood relationship with him. He has seen me grow into a teacher of my own weight and merit, a teacher making a name for himself with students who never knew there ever was an older Mr. Adams at the same campus. Francis Bacon once wrote, "We rise to great heights by a winding staircase." My life has constantly weaved towards and away from my father. And while it saddened me for many years that he encouraged me to weave away from him, he can now look at my short career and see different colors and contours than his. He taught English, not social studies. He never taught at a public university. I have been very fortunate to teach Political Science classes on a somewhat regular basis at the local California State University campus. He never presided over an Advanced Placement program or created a constitutional competition. I teach AP Government and Macroeconomics. He never won some of the teaching awards I have been fortunate to recently win. I mention these things not as a gesture of petty one-upmanship, only to demonstrate that although I too am a high school teacher, I have taken a walk very different from my father's.

I think he likes that. It's what he would have done.

Last year I was asked to speak at an event called "Principal Partnership Day." It's an event where members of the business community tour the local high schools to get a sense of what's going on in public classrooms. Before the business people depart to the different campuses, they eat breakfast and listen to a keynote speaker. In the middle of my speech I looked down at the front table at my father. For a moment the man who sought the perfect dog and regretted his son's career choice was gone—no smirk, no frown, no competitiveness. For that moment in time he was only a father smiling proudly, knowing that, although he was an extraordinary teacher, he was an even better father.

CHAPTER III
THE EARLY TEMPTATION

There is a temptation to look back at the convergence of three separate events at the outset of my teaching career and infer that a Providential hand was at work. I sometimes reminisce on the months following my college graduation and feel with ecclesiastic certainty that teaching was more than a career choice; it was a calling.

The first event was a phone call.

My plan for the fall after graduation was a simple one: substitute-teach during the day, take credential classes at night. I was prepared for a whirlwind year of beginning my career, working towards a social studies credential, and planning for a wedding the next summer. My fiancé was in her third year of law school at Santa Clara University so there would be few distractions during the week. Two weeks before the school year began I received a phone call from my former high school speech and debate coach. She was undergoing surgery and needed a two-week substitute to begin the school year. She taught freshmen-level English.

I jumped at the opportunity to open the school year. I wasn't their real teacher and I was in someone else's classroom. But I didn't care. Although my major was government, I felt more than capable of teaching literature to high school freshmen. In fact, I had to give serious thought about what I wanted to teach. My formal education was in government and economics, yet I had taken a number of classes in philosophy. My passion was in the social sciences but I was eager to begin my career in the humanities.

I remember watching the students file into the classroom on the first day. It had only been eight years since I attended my first day of high school. I don't remember much about my own first day, but I am certain I looked lost and over-whelmed. On the first day of class they looked so young, so miniature, so distant from my current station in life. They appeared more nervous about being students than I felt about being their newly-minted teacher. When the bell rang, a disconcerting and palpable silence reigned over the classroom.

What sticks out in my mind's eye after a decade, however, is a single period from that first week. It was the first class period I ever taught that was genuinely worthy of some pride. I spent an entire period attempting to explain why we read literature. As fourteen-year-olds, they had spent the better part of a decade redundantly reading stories either for amusement or, more likely, as an exercise in improving reading comprehension in order to perform well on a standardized exam. I was surprised to learn that none of the students saw in literature anything the least bit instructive or didactic, nothing beyond the minutiae of rote recall and regurgitation. It was a revelation to them that literature possesses a viewpoint or an opinion about the one thing it is important to have an opinion about: what is means to be a thinking and

sentient being. I tried to teach them Hemingway's Iceberg
Theory of Literature. (By the end of the year, my students
were desperately tired of my commandment to 'go beneath
the iceberg'). I tried to convince them that reading stories
can be a very serious business with serious implications for
the people we ultimately become.

"Are we realists or romantics?" I asked. "Fatalists of de-
terminists? Do we feel interconnected to something beyond
ourselves or are we alone in a universe defined by chaos?"

Most of the time I was the recipient of blank stares and
furrowed eyebrows. In retrospect, it wasn't just a bit much,
it was the equivalent of lighting a fire when all I needed was
a tiny spark. In their defense, the freshmen textbook was not
filled with the stuff of high literature and classical canonical
content. We weren't engaging in high-minded dialectics on
the ruminations of Proust or the lyric poetry of Sappho. We
were reading "The Lady or The Tiger." Surprisingly, it provided fertile ground for a discussion about the role of chance
in life and the content of justice. By the end of the first week,
I had arrived at two life-altering decisions: First, I loved the
classroom. Second, I was in despair about already being half
done with the long-term substitute assignment. I was not
looking forward to braving the storms of being a full-time
substitute teacher. Substitute teaching tends to be glamor-
ized babysitting, at times, and I remember how substitute
teachers were treated when I was a high school student.
They were routinely ignored, disrespected, and made the
fodder of teenage cruelty. On more than one occasion I
remember feeling sorry for them. And now I was about to
join their under-appreciated legion. It was a price I was willing to pay to become a teacher. However, I was definitely not
looking forward to it. I braced myself for an experience that
resembled something between basic military training and
fraternity hazing.

Then the second event intervened.

I began teaching in California in the late 1990's. Budgetary times were good and there was a state mandate that all freshmen English and math classes were to have no more than twenty two-students in them. This was known as 'classroom reduction.' I am a big fan of this policy even though it has rarely applied to me in eight years of teaching social studies where I am used to classes of thirty-five students or more. This mandate created a demand for additional English and math teachers. To my great fortune, the principal of Bakersfield High School happened to walk by my classroom one day when the door was standing open. I have no idea what I was saying or how I was saying it on that particular day, but apparently it hatched the idea in his brain that I should be hired to help fill the shortage of English teachers. Maybe he walked by during the one period of quality teaching I can recall during that first week. I'll never know. Having my own classroom and having my own students was more than I could have hoped for in this first year. Most aspiring social studies or English teachers have to go through student teaching. I was eager to avoid this process by having a class all to my own. It was an enchanting possibility.

I must admit, however, that teaching at the same high school where I graduated from just four years earlier had its odd moments. It took me a long time to start calling my former teachers by their first names. I also learned to wear a shirt and tie to school everyday, not only to comply with the rules of professional behavior, but because I was tired of having to show my classroom key to the campus security guards who refused to believe I was actually a teacher.

My first classroom was in the basement of the Science Building. The Science Building is located on the outer edge of the Bakersfield High School campus next to the PE fields. Soccer balls and screaming kids interrupted many a class session by crashing against the windows. The room was half sunk into the ground—when the windows rattled the entire class looked up at the top window. It was an odd place to teach English classes, but it was one of the only classrooms available since the school year was already three weeks old. I would turn on the lights every morning and watch the roaches flee for their safe crevices. The students called it "The Titanic Room" because the ceiling looked like the deck of the Titanic after it had been at the bottom of the ocean for ninety years. (It has since been remodeled, of course). There were no desks, only tables where the students could sit three wide. The one thing I liked about the classroom was that it was isolated. Very rarely did stray students walk by my classroom door. Except for the PE students, it was quiet because it had been forgotten by the administration and ignored by everyone except for my students. The only other classroom in the basement was the photo classroom and the photo students never walked down the hallway far enough to see what we were doing.

By current standards, the level of trust bestowed upon me by the school and the administration was extraordinary. I had absolutely no experience or formal training. All I was given for direction was a simple course of study that denoted the various topics I should cover during the school year and roughly how long I should spend on each item. I wasn't told which stories, plays, poems, and essays to teach. It wasn't mandated that I do exactly what other teachers in my department were doing. There was no educational Big Brother orchestrating my every movement and activity. There were no test scores upon which to evaluate my performance. I was given a rough outline of expectations and trusted to do my job. Looking back on it, this was a paradigm of trust that frankly does not exist today. Newly-hired teachers are now micro-managed, mentored, and monitored to ensure complete fidelity to the standards set forth by the state of California.

As a result of this trust, I constantly experimented with the curriculum and pedagogy of the class. My class was not formulaic in its conception or robotic in its execution. Some assignments and class activities were roaring successes. One of these included giving the students the first line of a story, i.e. a prompt, and requiring them to write their own short story from there. Another lesson used Platonic theories of beauty to help explain the power and poignancy of poetry.

Some were colossal failures. Nothing I did while reading *Great Expectations* seemed to work. Instead of referring to the protagonist as "Pip," the boys kept calling him "Pimp." It's upsetting to know that most of the time it was genuinely accidental on their part. "Pimp," I suppose, is just a natural component of their vernacular. *Romeo & Juliet* didn't go over particularly well, either. I finally broke down and let them watch Franco Zeffirelli's film version of it. There is a brief nude scene where Juliet's chest is on full display. I told the students I was going to fast-forward the video to avoid the nudity. The boys hissed and the girls laughed. I advanced the tape far past the offending scene—or so I thought. I restarted the film at the precise place where Juliet is seen in all her glory. Instead of hissing, this time the teenage boys spontaneously broke into cheers and hoots with their fists pumping high in the air. I imagined twenty conversations around the dinner table that evening. I was ready for a slew of parent phone calls and complaints. I was far from tenure and this was the last thing I needed on my short resume. One of the students could sense my dread. He came up after class and told me this was nothing in comparison to some of the other things they'd seen both in and out of other classrooms. As he was leaving, however, he turned around and said, "That doesn't mean it wasn't the best two seconds I've ever had in a class, though."

The other bundle of memories from my first semester teaching English came from a very different class than the ones I have been describing. All of my classes but one were college prep classes. College prep is not the highest level, but it is generally filled with bright kids who eventually end up attending college. My second period class was a "fundamental" level course. Most of the problems I have encountered in the classroom are associated with faulty learning dispositions, defective study skills, or the culture *writ large*. Never before had I encountered behavior as the primary hurdle of classroom success. Most of the students didn't bring a pencil or paper. I had to keep a classroom set of textbooks or else no one would have a book during class. Around Halloween, one student took a miniature pumpkin from my desk and decided to throw it against the ground to see if something that small would explode. Another student told me to "go fuck" myself because I asked him why he was missing so much class lately.

In some ways, I was clueless beyond description. One young man in this class was tardy everyday. Tardiness is common for first period, but not second. He hobbled in everyday with a lethargic gait and violently plopped himself down on his chair. He wasn't mean or aggressive or even particularly disrespectful. He constantly had dark red eyes and would listlessly sit through class everyday. Eventually, I began asking him if he had bad allergies. Was he wearing contact lenses that irritated his eyes? Was he getting enough sleep? He didn't seem to mind my inquiries. He just shrugged and the other students giggled.

Finally, in an attempt to end my ignorance, one of the girls came up to me after class one day and asked, "Mr.

Adams, are you trying to be funny by asking him all those questions?"

"No, I just don't understand what his problem is. Clearly there is one."

"He's high," she said, almost angrily.

"High?" I said, "On what?"

"Oh my God, Mr. Adams! On marijuana! Are you for real? Who are you?"

This was the one class period of my teaching career where every single day a student would ask the same question: "Mr. Adams, are we doing anything today?" They didn't ask what we were going to do, just if we were going to do anything at all. At first, this made me wonder what kind of classes they had been attending (or not attending). To hear it from them, there were plenty of days in plenty of classes where they just sat there. Finally, sometime in the second quarter, I lost my patience. I decided to teach them a lesson.

"If you want a day of doing nothing," I angrily said, "then we will do nothing. And I really mean nothing. No headphones! No magazines! No slouching! No sleeping on the desk! Sit there at attention and stare at nothing. That's the only option."

I sat at my desk grading papers for about thirty minutes, ever-confident in my power to teach them a lesson about the misplaced celebration of doing nothing. For me it would be torturous. I assumed it would also be painful for them. I have to give them credit. They followed my directions perfectly. They truly did nothing. After about thirty minutes I jumped up to my lectern.

"OK kiddies…..still want to do nothing? It's not fun, is it?" I asked.

Their response was not what I expected or wanted. There was a ringing and universal endorsement for more

time allotted to "doing nothing." One of the kids—for all I
know it could have been the young man with red eyes or the
one who told me to "fuck off"—told me this was the best
period of the year thus far. It was a bad dream that could
have been a scene right out of *Saved By The Bell* or *Head of
the Class*.

Ironically, this one period taught me more about teaching than I ever taught them about literature and writing.
What they taught me is the most poignant and important
lesson I will ever take from a classroom. It is true that my
day to day memories of this class are the anecdotes of their
outrageous behavior. But looked at from askance, what they
taught me was that even in a low-level class, even in a class
populated by students with little respect for teachers and no
curiosity for learning, there is the occasional student who
genuinely wants to learn. They are not always the boisterous
and gregarious types. They weren't the ones doing drugs and
telling their teacher to fuck off. Indeed, if I were to acquiesce
to their requests to do nothing everyday, I doubt any of them
would complain. I wouldn't receive any parent phone calls.
But I distinctly remember a quiet young lady from this fundamental class who would stay after class everyday to ask an
additional question or two. She brought paper. She brought
a pencil. Ultimately, she was a fierce reminder that even if a
class only has one student who wants to learn, that student
should be motivation enough for a teacher's best efforts.
Some of them understand the fundamental and practical
truth about education: it is often the only avenue out of a bad
situation. In a sea of bad fortune—violent backgrounds, difficult family situations, under-achieving schools—sometimes
education serves as a life raft.

I don't recall a single name from that class, just an
ever-shifting mental panorama of their faces and behavior.
They are now twenty-four years old, two years older than I

was when I tried to teach them. I don't know how many of them made it to graduation four years later. But I do wonder where they are now. At some point in life the option of doing nothing no longer remains a romantic aspiration. And even if dormancy remains attractive for a young person, it has no practical application in the real world. I remember asking them once, "What will become of all of you?" I didn't need autodidacts, but I couldn't relate to students who couldn't see beyond the seductive immediacy of now. Didn't they realize that tomorrow is married to today? Somewhere, out in the world, there are answers to my questions. These answers are, in fact, somewhere out in the world living and breathing as I write these very words about them. I wish I could say I had confidence that all of them turned it around. I wish I could say that life, being the greatest teacher of all, finally awakened them to the harsh truth that a journey taken without regard for tomorrow tends to be exceptionally difficult and empty.

A few weeks into my new job it came to my attention that I might not be able to keep my classes. The principal informed me that the district had discovered a "credentialing problem." To receive an emergency credential in English the state of California required that I take a certain number of "upper-division" courses in English. Washington & Lee didn't make the distinction between upper and lower division courses in the same manner as the Cal State system. In the California system, lower division courses were 100 and 200 level. Upper division was 300 and 400. Washington & Lee only went up to the 300's. Only internships and other non-conventional courses were designated as 400 level classes. I tried to explain this to the district office, but they resisted. The letter of the law was clear. This was the first time I sensed there was something remarkably amiss about the criteria for hiring new teachers. The principal wanted to hire me. The district wanted me to work for them. But my capacity to do the job well and true was absolutely irrelevant. The hiring system was designed for teachers who were educated at state universities, not for recent graduates from an east coast liberal arts college.

I finally took my cause to the local California State University campus (the same place where I was taking credentialing courses at night and would later become an adjunct lecturer in the Political Science Department), hoping they would agree to the notion that 200 level courses at W&L were the equivalent of upper division courses in the California State University system. I remember standing in the School of Education riddled with deep despair. I was on the brink of losing my position. I pleaded with the secretary to understand my situation. She told me the only chance I had was to go to the English department chairman. But, she said, he wasn't going to sign my form. I was going to have to take more classes if I wanted the emergency credential.

This was the last of three providential events.

On my walk to the English department, I went over the arguments in my mind. I was going to be charming and courteous to whomever I encountered, not desperate and outraged as was my want. I had my transcript and equivalency form in hand. But in my heart I knew that it was hopeless. I was going to lose my English classes. I was going to have to wait another year and go through the arduousness of student teaching, and all because my college alma mater had an odd system of denoting its courses.

I knew the chances were slim that he would sign it. It was a long shot. Any English department chairman working in Bakersfield, California was going to be ignorant of how they do things at a small liberal arts college in the middle of Virginia. In all likelihood, he had never heard of the place. When I entered the department chairman's office, he was at his computer typing away. I remember thinking this cramped office was a far cry from the spacious and wood paneled offices at W&L. He barely had enough room for two chairs. He was an elderly man with one of the kindest faces I have ever witnessed. I later learned that he had been at Cal State, Bakersfield from the time it opened in the early 1970's.

I didn't know how to begin my exegesis. Should I introduce myself? Should I simply tell him my problem without the details or drama of it all? I decided to start from the very beginning and keep it simple. I began with the root of the problem. I breathed in heavily.

"Have you ever heard of Washington & Lee University?" I asked, trying to gauge the level of difficulty I was about to encounter. He looked a little confused at first. "It's in Virginia," I added.

He swerved around in his seat, suddenly very interested in the question.

"Why yes," he said. "I know exactly where it is. I graduated from there almost forty years ago. Why would you ask?"

I am not sure how involved Providence is in the lives of ordinary people. I would like to think that prayer makes a difference. But at that moment I felt the mighty hand of something—perhaps God, perhaps Chance. I might as well have won the lottery.

For the next hour we had a wonderfully animated conversation reminiscing about W&L. I told him about the shenanigans of the current fraternities. He told me what it was like in the days before W&L went co-ed. Since I had just graduated three months earlier, he had plenty of questions for me. Most people on the West Coast have never heard of the place, much less possess an appreciation for it. At the end of our talk, he signed my form and I was granted an emergency credential in English from the California Commission on Teacher Credentialing.

By Thanksgiving I saw myself making small strides towards success in the classroom. Parent Night was nerve-racking but positive. (A parent tried to set me up with an older daughter!) First quarter grades were shockingly low but I gradually began to understand how to positively push my students to do more than they were accustomed to. But it was on Thanksgiving Day that I finally began to recognize that my decision to enter the classroom was no mistake. That evening after waking up from a tryptophan-induced nap, I casually checked my email. There was a message waiting for me from a student in my 6th period class. She was a very good student and heavily vocal in class. I couldn't imagine why she was emailing me on Thanksgiving Day. I clicked on her message.

She wrote to tell me about a specific Thanksgiving family tradition practiced in her household. After the communal prayer everyone at the table was supposed to list something they were thankful for during that particular year. I don't know what the standard answers sounded like—maybe health, maybe a business deal going well, who knows? But I instantly began to blush when she explained what she was thankful for: she was thankful for being in my class. It was the type of email teachers print out and put away in a drawer somewhere to read in their retirement.

Instead, I simply thought to myself, "how nice," and promptly deleted it. Most cynics would chalk it up as an episode of extreme but highly original ass-kissing. But this particular student was going to receive a decent grade with or without the assistance of an ass-kissing email. At the time, it was certainly the kindest sentiment a student had ever expressed to me.

Since then I have come to fully appreciate the gesture because I have learned over ten years that it is antithetical to the natural proclivity of the teenage mind. Virtually all American teenagers face their good fortune in life as being a natural component of a functioning world. Of course, they think to themselves, we have food in our stomachs, clothes on our backs, and immunization records on file. Of course gravity exists and the speed of light is 3.0×10^8 m/s. That's just life. That's just the world. Right? But this young lady was articulating something more grandiose than a simple "thank you." She was using the occasion of Thanksgiving to give voice to the fact that she was the beneficiary of something that is not necessarily natural or assumed. To her, having a good teacher was a privilege, not a misconstrued right.

Perhaps the universe sensed I was on the verge of an inflated ego and felt it had to be promptly deflated. Right around the time I received my blissful Thanksgiving email, my English classes went on hiatus for a week. The high school district mandated that every freshman take a class on abstinence and AIDS prevention. The teacher of this course took one look at my classroom and requested another classroom in a building across the PE fields in Spindt Hall. My only duty for the week included taking attendance at the beginning of each class period. After that I was free to leave and go back to my vacant classroom to plan for the next semester and catch up on some grading.

On the last day of the AIDS class, I walked across the PE fields after lunch to take attendance. I strolled across the field on a beautiful Friday afternoon thinking I would never have a week this easy ever again. I was looking forward to the drive up Interstate-5 later that afternoon to visit my fiancé. Suddenly, a few yards in front of me, two lanky freshmen faced each other with their fists held up in a boxer's position. They were clearly on the verge fighting. They both looked at me and ran into Spindt Hall. I giggled to myself that the tie and attendance folder obviously held great power over those who felt its mighty presence. It had just broken up a fight with its mere appearance. I was a high school teacher. I possessed gravitas.

This was so much better than going to law school or working in a cubicle somewhere.

When I opened up the doors to Spindt Hall, however, the same two boys were now fully immersed in an attack against one another. This time there wasn't the slightest glint of restraint. A real fight lacks humanity—it's animalism incarnate. These two fourteen year olds had thrown off the armaments of their humanity and I was walking into the middle of it. It turns out the folder and tie had only delayed the inevitable fight, not stopped it. I didn't panic. After all, I still had gravitas…right?

"Hey, stop it," I yelled with confidence, assuming, of course, that my reappearance would have the same arresting effect as before. But this time they didn't stop. They didn't flinch or even acknowledge that I was standing there. My presence was hollow and barren of any tincture of intimidation. Where was the gravitas from a moment before? Why did it vanish so suddenly? My colleagues and students later told me it was never there in the first place. I yelled louder this time, "Don't make me send you two to the dean. Come on, stop!"

This had the same level of success as the previous warning. I decided the only thing to do was to gently step between the two teens and push them away from each other. They were skinny fourteen-year-old kids. I was a beefy twenty-two-year-old teacher. This wouldn't be tough, I assumed.

Without looking, I took a small step between them at the precise moment when one of them was about to strike a lethal blow to the other's face. Instead of hitting the student, the punch inadvertently struck my left eye. Feeling disori-

ented and more than a little frustrated, I screamed out for a
PE coach to come and deal with the problem. There was a
cut below my left eye and I was later brought into the office
to identify the two students involved in the altercation. The
principal called me in to his office and told me I could go
home for the day. Although this is the same man who hired
me and has been nothing but kind and generous to me ever
since, I got the distinct impression that he found the entire
situation a little bit amusing.

By Monday morning, I had a black eye protruding from
my face and there were rampant rumors around campus
that, "Young Mr. Adams got beat up by a freshman on Friday
afternoon." At lunch, my colleagues decided to show me
some techniques illuminating the finer points of head locks,
pressure points, and the like. For every fight technique that
was demonstrated, I had to listen to the accompanying story
about when it was used on a student, how the student react-
ed, and what I should do next time I encounter a fight.

Of course, I deplore physical violence and there never
was a next time. I know fellow teachers who eagerly await
the opportunity to break up a fight. But I always tell my
students—half jokingly, I guess—that if there is ever a melee
in my class, I will go get some popcorn and a soda before I
saunter over to the phone to call security, especially if it is
a fight between two female students. I tell this story to my
classes ten years later merely to amuse them. But at the time,
this incident hurt more than just my eye. I could handle the
rumors and stomach the embarrassment. What I remember most about the incident was the long drive up Northern
California that Friday afternoon. I got a two-hour head
start up the endlessly dull Interstate-5. A year ago, I thought
to myself while driving, I spent my days on a Eden-esque
campus reading classic literature and thinking big thoughts.
Now I was working in an inner-city high school and getting

my head beat in by teenagers half my size.

Maybe law school and the cubicle weren't such bad ideas after all.

Was this really what I wanted to do with my life? Did I really go into a profession where I had to deal with aggressive situations and encounter a school environment that was becoming increasingly vulgar and violent?

By April I was eager for the school year to end. I didn't enjoy being a student teacher in the mornings and my freshmen English classes in the afternoon were quickly becoming stale. They couldn't understand the phraseology of Dickens and it took weeks to read it in class. My black eye healed and the whispers that tarnished my pride eventually quieted down. I took the fight as an outlier, a chance encounter that I might not ever experience again. As long as there is the presence of youth and testosterone on a high school campus, I wagered, there will be conflict.

But my isolated encounter with violence is paltry in comparison to the macabre scenes broadcasted from Colorado that spring. I am not sure if the gruesome bloodbath that transpired at Columbine High School had a pernicious effect on every high school in America. At my high school there was little dialogue in the wake of the Columbine tragedy. Every teacher in America probably had a similar unspoken thought as we watched children dangling from library windows and grainy images of gunmen walking down school corridors: could this happen at my high school? Sadly, but not surprisingly, all of the members of the high school community became more sensitive to the possibility of violent intrusions. There was a heightened awareness in the community that no school is immune to the possibility of terror.

While Columbine proved to be a paradigm-shifting event in the psyche of secondary schools across America, there is something unsettling about the new marriage that now exists between schools and violence. This marriage has become increasingly common in the decade since I have entered the classroom, from the massive killings at Columbine and Virginia Tech to the sheer nauseating evil on display at the Amish school shooting in Bart Township, Pennsylvania. Academics, social commentators, and experts of every stripe have offered explanations about the upsurge of shootings in recent years. Much has been said and written about the similarities of the shootings, from the common ethnicity of the shooters to the tendency for these events to occur in upper-middle class suburbia.

It is true that learning in the midst of violence is nothing new. The Peloponnesian War occurred in the midst of The Golden Age of Greece. As C.S. Lewis noted in his essay "Learning in War Time," the Athens of Pericles didn't just give us the Parthenon, but the *Funeral Oration*. Learning and reading can even take place on the battlefield. German soldiers, for instance, veraciously read Friedrich Nietzsche's *Thus Spoke Zarathustra* in the midst of battle during World War I.

But there is a qualitative distinction between learning in the proximity of violence versus learning being interrupted by unforeseen violence. If there is any place in the world that is supposed to be isolated from the clutches of mayhem and violence, it is a public school classroom. This is a place that is ideally filled with the ambiance of youth. For such a haven to be invaded by the reality of sudden death and needless suffering is to impale the hope that any place in society can remain sacrosanct. There is something terrifying—primordial in its vitality—in watching the footage of young children and teenagers engage in a primal run to escape their schools in the hopes of securing survival. I literally shudder to imagine my own children or students being made to run in such a fashion.

But most of all, the residue of Columbine and the handful of other high school shootings is simple to describe: indescribable indignation. Violence and death are undeniable fixtures of the human condition. But the defining characteristic of any civilization that values civility is found in its effort to minimize the presence of violence in everyday life, especially for the most vulnerable. When a Hobbesian state of nature doesn't merely materialize on urban streets and in war zones, but in the most sacred and innocent of places, there is a raw and undeniable outrage that ought to build up within the walls of society's chest. Something has gone astray when the most inviolate of places becomes a target for blood and gore. As a child, I saw my school as a safe sanctuary exclusively devoted to the mind and human growth. Yet what has happened in the past ten years is truly tragic. We are now forced to mentally combine the highest tenets of our humanity–thought, reason, learning—with that which is the most depraved and baleful. One gets the nagging sensation that all is not right with a culture which has no solution to such sinister symptoms of a more draconian disease. In our hearts—as teachers and as citizens—we feel undeniably stultified by this spectacle, with no words to explain it. We simply shrug. We merely feel baffled. We make plans and form committees to deal with the problem should it appear on our campus. Were we to turn on the television and see the familiar gruesome scenes we would again be horrified; but we wouldn't be surprised.

By the time the shock of Columbine began to recede, the demise of my first year was close at hand. I found myself in a reflective—albeit somewhat sour—mood that first spring. When my father once exclaimed that, "good teachers are born, not made," he wasn't referring to the implementation of one particular educational theory of education. He was alluding to something more personal, more basic about the human being occupying the front of the classroom. As I finished student-teaching and credential classes, I was left to conclude that a teaching credential can empower a teacher to be well organized and decently prepared, but it cannot make a teacher affable and kind, knowledgeable and patient, humorous and approachable. Modern educational research bears this out. The premise that completing education courses and passing a standardized content exam translates into proficient teaching is highly questionable. The rich spectrum of habits that translates into quality teaching cannot be mechanistically chiseled into the inner-marble of a teacher. This animating virtue, of course, is passion—passion for the subject being taught and a love for the students and their futures. Passion in the classroom is a benign communicable germ. Passion from the teacher disrupts the regimentation that plagues most high school classrooms. Passion is what fuels any educational theory of merit. Without passion there is no education, no elation, no promise of anything beyond the mundane.

Anecdotally, some of the finest education systems in the world approach the task of teacher recruitment in a radically different manner than we Americans. Finland generally weighs mastery of a subject as the highest criteria for hiring a potential teacher. That is why most teachers have Masters Degrees in Finland. It is a fair assumption that individuals who obtain a Masters possess both a high level of interest and knowledge about the subject they have studied. After all, how many college professors are ever subjected to the splendors of a credentialing process? Their capacity for instruction is built solely on the assumption of subject mastery. How backwards are our priorities when possessing a Master's Degree can be a liability to getting hired because a school district would have to pay a higher salary? I will never forget a guest speaker in one of my credentialing classes who was the head of hiring for the district I now work in. Someone asked, "What is the best way to get hired? Should we have teaching experience, a Master's Degree, come from a prestigious college?" The speaker looked him straight in the face and deadpanned, "Coach a sport."

Perhaps the entire process of teacher readiness and hiring is predicated on the faulty and specious assumption that those who possess teaching credentials are the most qualified to teach young people. Consider that few of the students who attend elite colleges in this country actually consider a career in the public classroom. And yet we readily acknowledge that a person with a Ph.D. is, *ipso facto,* prepared to teach college students. American colleges are the finest in the world. As many newspaper columnists and social scientists of substance have noted, the quality of American colleges has attracted an army of fecundate mental capital from all over the world. These foreigners-turned-Americans are largely responsible for the technological advantages we enjoy over the rest of the world. Clearly, American college students are not suffering because their professors were never forced to take a year of their life to obtain a subject-matter teaching credential. How different is it to suggest that a young person graduating from Berkeley or Bates, UCLA or Notre Dame, is fully equipped with the knowledge for quality secondary teaching? The Hamilton Project—a think-tank aligned with the Brookings Institute—penned a paper on teacher credentialing a few years back that succinctly captured the point: "To put it simply, teachers vary considerably in the extent to which they promote student learning, but whether a teacher is certified or not is largely irrelevant to predicting his or her effectiveness."

I am saddened by the fact that few, if any, of my childhood and college friends who attended wonderful American universities considered entering the public school classroom.

Most of them have become successful professionals and academics ranging from air force pilots and investment bankers to English professors and insurance agents. Most people have to learn to become a teacher without making any money. My friends decided to use their educations to attend law, medical or graduate school. Some entered careers ripe with the prospect for advancement. It's not that America doesn't need good doctors and academics, but what we do need is a generation of transformative public school teachers who can harness their intellect and education to the betterment of the country. It is a quixotic and highfalutin aspiration, I acknowledge. These recent graduates might well discover after a few years that they want to take their fancy degrees and sharp minds elsewhere. Perhaps teaching isn't for them. But at least they will have devoted a few years of their life to hundreds of young people who will benefit from the experience. This is the idea behind programs such as Teach For America. Nobody is ever going to get rich or famous by spending his or her days in a public school. Yet there is a special form of delight that is reserved for those who dare to share the content of their minds with others.

As a matter of fact, when I look back at the first few years of my teaching career, I sometimes believe I was a better teacher at twenty-three than I now am at thirty-two. It's not that my classes were of a higher quality, it's that I was more receptive to the contemplation of improvement. At twenty-three I didn't know what worked and what didn't. I fully expected failure to occur on a somewhat regular basis. I wasn't touchy about disappointments or resistant to negative critiques about my teaching. When a lesson or lecture didn't work, I filed it away into the inner-recesses of my brain as needing revision or perhaps complete abandonment. But with age comes the prickly bravado of delusional expertise. I have begun to adopt a veteran's logic of teaching: I have

taught the same lesson or given the same lecture for many
years. Therefore, it works.

Though fewer of my classes flop than when I was a
young teacher, in the early days of my career I was more
likely to embrace the best advice I ever received about teaching. A family friend, who was a long-time teacher, told me,
"Don't be afraid to make a fool of yourself to make an important point." I am happy to say that I lived up to this high-
minded advise many times in my early career. I heartily
embraced the realm of the silly and sophomoric if it helped
make a point or demonstrated a concept. I even agreed to
participate in the asinine skits they want new teachers to
join in during school rallies. This included a chicken eating
contest, a solo interpretive dance with Britney Spears blar-
ing in the background and doing circles on my back on the
gymnasium floor as my favorite song from college, ABBA's
Dancing Queen, blared from the speakers—all this, I might
add, in front of over a thousand students and staff in the
school gymnasium.

In my first few years there was an urgency, almost a
ferocity, to my classes, a ferocity that seems to have been
tamed nowadays to a middle-age throb of gentle enthusiasm.
I remember receiving the teenage equivalent of accolades in
abundance. Teenagers rarely say that you made them think
or that they enjoyed looking at something in a new way.
What they say is that they "enjoy" the class. It is the apogee
of praise for a teenager to comment that he or she actually
looks forward to coming to class everyday.

In these early years I experienced a rich constellation
of sensations, ranging from dejection to something I never
knew was possible until I became a teacher. What I am
alluding to is the stuff of a poet, not the literary terrain a
simple high school teacher. And yet, there seem so be moments in a classroom—cruelly rare, I would add—where all

the components of time and space seem to perfectly align themselves so that transcendence feels as though it were close at hand, when inspiration is more than a word, when the teacher and students and content seem to become one combustible mass of mutual understanding. Every single student in the classroom is paying perfect attention. There are no distractions. I say exactly what I want to say in just the way I want it to be said.

I remember the first time the teaching gods granted me such a moment...

We were studying one of my favorite poems, *George Gray*, which is about a man who never experienced any of the things in life he longed for—love, success, triumph—because he was afraid to take any risks. This degenerated into a riff about the necessity of deep consideration about what my students should want out of their lives, that life is too rich and pregnant with possibilities to settle for the mundane and humdrum of mediocrity. Of course, at the time I was more eloquent and concise. I had a captive audience. They knew and I knew that we were engaged in more than meditations of dry information and meaningless facts. We were talking about their lives, their journeys, their potential to become a better type of human being as a result of having read *George Gray*.

As I look back on my early days as a teacher, I know (or at least I feel) that those moments were more frequent and, alas, more genuine. There are now days when I drive to work hoping that some comment or some thought will give birth to the wonder of a moment similar to what I have just described. In the past few years, I don't know where these moments have gone. I have some suspicions which will be explored elsewhere. Perhaps they are still present in my classes, but they no longer carry the virginal gloss of spontaneity as they once did in the early years of my career.

At the end of my first year, my student teacher evalua-
tor, an old man who had been retired for years, came up to
me after observing one of my classes and said, "I loved your
class, especially the stuff about Socrates. But you're going to
have to learn to teach in a different way."

When I asked why, he said, "Because when you're not
twenty-two you won't have the energy to jump around the
room like that. You'll want them to do some of the work.
Don't be tempted to make yourself the center of the classroom experience."

And that was the early temptation: making myself the
center of the classroom experience.

I never recognized my deficiency until that moment.
Subconsciously, I felt that I could will my interest and energy
into the hearts and minds of my students. If they liked me,
then they would like the class. If I entertained them, then
they would listen to the content of my lessons. If they cared
about what I thought they would surely work hard in order
to avoid disappointing me. This was the gravest mistake
from my early years. I had unconsciously made the classroom about me, not about them. I did not do this because I
wanted their applause or laughs. It wasn't about ego.

I did it because I had a stealth agenda about what I was
trying to accomplish with the limited amount of time I had
with them. In every piece and form of literature we studied,
(and later in my career, within every historical time period
we mastered) there was a subtle subtext to what I wanted
my students to learn. I wanted them to use the magic of the
classroom to understand that there are schemes of grandeur
that are only accessible to those with a reflective disposition.
I wanted them to learn that to live fully doesn't require us to
champion the beast within, only to reflect on what is highest and possible in each of us. I wanted them to know that a
moral life, a life that is not immune to the highest aspirations

of our humanity, is one to which we should all aspire.

I wanted them to know my definition of good teaching: a good teacher is one whose teaching matters beyond the doors of a classroom. To divorce learning from life is to misunderstand the entire function of education. One need only to take an elementary perusal of the great works on education, from books like Plato's *Republic* and Rousseau's *Émile*, to the masterful essays on education by the likes of John Locke or Montaigne. In every canonical instance, to live is to learn.

But this understanding was forgotten a few years later. The teacher who left college viewing education as a quasi-religious activity of the mind was gone and in its place is now something very different, more mechanistic, less youthful.

In a word, more standard.

INTERLUDE ONE
A SON UNNAMED
(MARCH, 2000)

September beckons and so I remember: we didn't give him a name.

That is what haunts me. Even today. Even after all of these years.

I only saw him from afar and only for a few fleeting moments. His heart had stopped beating at least a week before our visit to the maternity ward. That's what the doctor told us. But now he was out of my wife's womb and laying on a blanket-laden counter next to the hospital-room sink.

My wife lay in her bed drifting in and out of a drug-altered consciousness. She had been cramping for hours in her hospital bed before we both fell asleep after the eleven o'clock news. Slowly—ever slowly, ever cruelly—the small bump vanished from under her stomach. The hospital had run out of chairs earlier in the day and I was left with only a

pillow and the brutality of the hospital floor. It was going to
be a long night. I was shaken from my slumber by the doctor's voice. It felt like only minutes had passed.

"Oh, it's just right here," the doctor uttered, softly, yet
still in a matter-of-fact, clinical tone. She wanted to avoid
rousing either of us from our sleep. She turned to the nurse
beside her. "We just need to get it out and clean her up. Let's
be quiet."

When I opened my eyes and sat up high enough to
orient myself, all I could see was the back of a nurse turn-
ing away from my wife, walking over to the towel on the
counter and setting down a mass of pink flesh: my son. He
wasn't passed into my arms the way I had always imagined
he would be. Nor were there the tears of relief that follow in
the wake of any successful pregnancy. All I was offered was
a stealth glimpse of him—nothing more than a pinkish blur.
Nothing distinct. Nothing resembling the baby I had always
imagined he'd be.

I knew my wife was awake because she violently turned
away. And I knew why. A few weeks earlier the gynecologist
had taken a picture of him in the womb. That first ultrasound picture was how she wanted to remember him. Even
today, if she looks at the picture, I can imagine the mental
chicanery transpiring in her mind's eye. She can momen-
tarily forget his fate. She can transport herself back to the
weeks that followed this first magical snapshot of our first
attempt at parenthood. In those weeks before the second
damning ultrasound, we can find solace in the fanciful illusion that he was healthy and growing, moving in the only
direction human time allows us to move: birth, life, death.
But my son had no real birth and he certainly didn't have a
life. All he had was a death. I saw her trace her finger over
the ultrasound picture many times, as though the smooth
glossy feel of the film somehow hinted at the softness of a

real baby's skin. It's been years since I've seen her look at the picture. It's tucked away in a place that only she knows about. I suspect she looks at it on occasion. Sometimes I want to look, but I don't want to broach the most sensitive of marital subjects.

It didn't occur to me at the time that I should stand up, walk over, and look at him. It was a short-sighted rejection—one that resonates with me to this day. "What kind of a man doesn't recognize his own son," I have chastised myself by saying. But the slight against him wasn't done with the veneer of shame or the forethought of malice. Only fear. Fear of ingraining that which can never be erased from a father's mind. Fear of seeing the blood and the fluid of an unsuccessful pregnancy. Fear of knowing the nuances and details of my child's fateful end.

He was only at four months gestation when his little heart inexplicably stopped beating. Maybe my wife is wise to preserve the image from the ultrasound as a paean to her hopes and maternal aspirations. But I'm not so easy to placate. And so, I do regret my retreat from his little, swollen body, even if the only authentic nourishment I could have garnered from looking at him was the harsh reality of his death. I have tried to go easy on myself these past few years. After all, I ask myself, what could I have possibly seen?

But the truth of the matter is that I would have seen a lot. At four months a fetus begins to grow eyebrows and eyelashes. He would have weighed almost four ounces. I would have seen his hands, his legs, and the contours of his nose. Yes, Promethean knowledge is knowledge that clarifies and captures the essence of the malady at hand and in the heart. Unfortunately for me, such knowledge is no longer available. I made my choice. I chose willful ignorance. I saw no eyebrows, no eyelashes, no appendages. A poor choice. A cowardly choice. A haunting choice.

I asked only two questions, simple questions, which startled the nurse who thought I was still sleeping beside the bed.

"What is it?"

"A boy," she said, flatly.

She answered me without meeting my gaze—a clear invitation to return to silence.

But I had to ask another: "What will you do with him?"

I could immediately tell that she didn't want to tell me the truth.

"We have a small crematorium for situations like this." This time she kept eye contact, waiting for yet another question. But I had nothing to ask. Nothing to say. And unfortunately for me, I was infected with paternal paralysis.

The rest of the morning was a blur, except for the clueless hospital worker who kept calling my wife "mom" as she signed the discharge papers.

No name. No glance. No funeral. No acknowledgment that he ever occupied a place in the fabric of time. I could have given him such an acknowledgment in my own, albeit, minimal way. But I balked at the opportunity. He lives on, but not as he should; not as a name or as a visual memory, but as the residue of the strongest guilt I have ever felt in my life. And now, after all of these years, I cannot forgive myself because to do such a thing would be to relinquish the only kernel of proof that he ever existed. As the years have worn on, I find that I need my guilt. I need to feel the splinters of regret.

Maybe that's why I am quick to dismiss the reflexive religiosity that tries to take away the pain by telling me that he is with God, in heaven, in the clutches of a paradise that exceeds human comprehension. I know there is a passage in the Bible, Jeremiah 1:15, that says, "I knew you before I formed you in your mother's womb." But I remain skeptical.

And I say that as a devout, God-fearing, believing Christian. The riches of eternal life are only riches if you have tasted the splendors of life itself. They are only riches if you have known what it is to love and be loved; only riches if you understand what it means to grow old and to see the things you love the most in this world whither and eventually disappear; only riches if you have struggled with faith in a world where it sometimes makes more sense not to believe in a divine order of things. But he never experienced any of these things. What would heaven mean to such a soul?

It would be filial sedition for me to suggest that there is not a divine element to the creation of a human life. After all, twenty-four years earlier my father made a daily ritual of stopping at a Catholic Church on his way to work every morning to make my four brothers and sisters (all adopted by my father) file out of the car in order to light a candle for their unborn sibling. They probably wondered why any of this was necessary. No one lit any candles on their behalf, they wagered, yet they all made it safely to their teenage years. One of them once remarked that they lit a candle praying they wouldn't have to light any more candles. My father was quick to remind them that they were not the inhabitants of a forty-year old womb. And this was in 1976—long before it became vogue or fashionable for Hollywood starlets to have children in their mid-40's, long before the revolution in fertility drugs and treatments. Having a child at forty in the 1970's was something of a dangerous proposition.

My father once joked that he saw four sons in my future, all with names that start with "J," and more importantly, last names that were to be carried into the future and multiplied. You see, he was an only child and I was his only biological son. His hopes for immortality rested squarely on my reproductive shoulders. I come from a hodge-podge of personalities and legacies that is only possible in America. I am descended from a line of educators, Civil War soldiers, slave-owners, coal miners, farmers, staunch Catholics, reluctant believers, and probably more importantly, men. After all, we do hold the seeds to life, women's liberation aside, and there is absolutely nothing that can be done about it. The hope of a grandson was an eternal hope for my father—a hope that vanished for many years. My father is too good a man to say how much it saddened him. And to be fair, he loves my two daughters so much he was probably a little ashamed of his sadness. But I know it bothered him.

The saga of candle lighting continues to this day. Every church service my father attends, Sundays as well as religious holidays, he lights a candle for my son that never was. He finally told me, just this year, what his words are when he looks up at a stylized crucified Christ: "I won't forget you." I am sure he is sorry for the Christmas presents his grandson never opened, for the light that never shone in his eyes. He's sorry for the joy that was never given to my wife and me at that point in our lives. Most of all, I'm sure he's sorry that my son never saw a dawn and that he never held his hand.

My wife was comforted by the words of our Indian doctor who told us that in her culture this was merely a sign that we weren't supposed to be his parents, that his birth—his existence—was never in peril. He had simply moved on to explore other options. While my wife could bear the notion that he was somewhere else in some other form exploring "other options," I'm afraid it didn't comfort me. If all these years later the order of the universe somehow dropped him into another womb to be born in another place; if, today, he is somewhere in the world breathing air, thinking thoughts, and emoting emotion, then in no way do I have any claim of being his father.

Heaven? Reincarnation? Perhaps they are real. But not for my son. No. I'll take my guilt as the anchor of his existence.

I would have named him Jeffrey and called him Jeff.

That is, if I had walked across the hospital room that early spring morning and named him. His due date was September first and he would be approaching his ninth birthday this fall. Despite my extraordinary fortune in this life—a wonderful wife, two beautiful daughters, and a teaching career I genuinely cherish—I find myself in early September staring out my third floor classroom window at the beautiful trees whose green leaves are on the cusp of darkening to a solemn autumn brown. My thoughts turn to what might have been. I wonder what he would have looked like. Would he have my insecurity or his mother's zest for perfection in all things; my crooked nose or his mother's miniature chin? Would he have been the tennis prodigy I hoped him to be? These are tormenting questions because they are like all questions of real consequence in life: they are unanswerable. I wish in many ways that I could simply give a nihilist shrug to all of my concerns and simply acknowledge that life isn't always fair and that not everything happens for a reason. Things happen. People react. The only tragedy lies with those who can't learn to move on.

So maybe that's what this is: a point of departure, a chance to move on. Indeed, I suppose this paternal exegesis has little to do with Jeffrey and everything to do with me. Because like it or not, none of my options allow me to do what I really want to do. No matter if he is with God, reincarnated as someone else, or simply biological nothingness and thus completely non-existent, he won't be able to hear or relate to any of this. But if there was some way, some shrouded mystery of the universe that would transubstantiate itself and allow a father to say something to a son he never knew and who, in all honesty, perhaps never really existed at all, I would use it to convey the simplest of fatherly messages.

Jeffrey: I'm so sorry.

PART II
REALITY STRIKES (2000-2006)

CHAPTER IV
STANDARDIZING THE
EXTRAORDINARY

—

❝If you want to become truly great students," I sometimes suggest to my World History students, "you should mimic the intellectual adventures of Petrarch."

They look at me with gazes betwixt wonderment and annoyance. I always utter these words during the first quarter of the school year before the students really know me. They don't know if I am a step away from quirky or, more likely, just not a flavor they're used to.

Why do I attempt to seamlessly fuse a Renaissance academic and poet with the educational aspirations of modern American high school students?

They don't often mingle, I admit.

Petrarch trudged through the roads of Europe at the dawn of the Renaissance looking for the lost texts of antiquity. He visited dozens of libraries and monasteries in search of Greek and Latin texts that had been ignored for the better part of a millennium. Of course, there was already the rediscovery of Aristotle's work in Toledo, Spain and in other Middle Eastern Universities. These discoveries of 'The Philosopher' served as the genesis for an entire corpus of scholarship—think Abelard, Anselm and Aquinas—that attempted to reconcile the dominion of a Christian God with the mechanistic world-view of the Ancient Greek. This didn't much matter to Petrarch who preferred Platonic idealism to the cold, disembodied theories of Aristotle.

I often romanticize Petrarch's treacherous journey for my students. He was a man with a soaring intellect but a bruised heart, having been endlessly rebuffed by "Laura," the amorous inspiration for much of his poetry. I tell my students to imagine what it was like to be the man who rediscovered the weighty ideas and advanced learning of the Greeks and Romans. These are ideas, I explain, that had not occupied any European's brain for almost a thousand years. Akin to Galileo being the first human to see the craters on the moon or the rings of Saturn, here was Petrarch basking in the literary treasures of Virgil, the history of Livy, the Stoicism of Seneca and Cicero. The monks who copied these texts for hundreds of years in the midst of the Dark Ages likely had no appreciation of what it was they were copying.

Petrarch never knew what intellectual worlds would flow from his latest literary acquisition. Sometimes these worlds were profound; sometimes they were simply beyond his comprehension. But whatever he encountered, he did so with intellectual humility. He was so ravenous for more texts and more learning that by the end of his life he had acquired one of the largest libraries in all of Europe. In essence, he was the Italian version of Thomas Jefferson.

I quickly tone down the rhetoric before they start looking at each other with raised eyebrows and suspicious glances. I spell it out in simple terms for my fifteen-year-olds.

"Shouldn't Petrarch's journey be an example for the rest of you to follow when you come to school everyday? Petrarch didn't know what he would uncover in the next church, library, or monastery he entered. Likewise, you don't know what will be encountered on a daily basis. Sometimes you are overwhelmed by what you learn. And yes, sometimes it's painful to stretch your intellectual wings in a subject you have little capacity for. When I was in high school, Algebra might as well have been Greek. Well, for Petrarch, it actually was Greek!"

This is the juncture when I can tell the cynics from the optimists—some students are clay, others are marble, but they can all be formed into something finer through their contact with big ideas and important historical events. What I teach my students is nothing as rich as the texts of antiquity. Still, the validity of the question remains: shouldn't an idealized form of education be extraordinary? Shouldn't the classroom—at its highest and best form—become a cerebral Mecca of thinking thoughts heretofore unconsidered by its students? Don't we want an education system in which students can take delight in the process of self-discovery?

I ask these questions in the midst of an educational era that has wholly invested itself in outcome-based education (OBE), an idea that is not completely new to this era but has resulted in a seismic pedagogic shift in the course of my teaching career. As I detailed in the previous chapter, at the outset of my career I was given a course of study and trusted to do a good job teaching the students. This was—from my perspective—implicit encouragement to experiment, innovate, and refine my lessons and teaching methods.

About five years into my career, however, the arena within which teachers work and operate began to change. More concisely, it began to shrink. Slowly by slowly state legislators, district leaders, and school administrators began to act *in loco parentis* by instituting policies that slowly eroded the autonomy of the teacher to follow the course of study in his or her own manner and pace.

It is ironic but appropriate that Petrarch coined the phrase "dark ages" because this seismic pedagogic shift is its educational equivalent.

What I am referring to, of course, is the advent of standardized education. On its face, education has always been standardized. Standardization movements began long ago. School boards and state legislators have always articulated—sometimes broadly, sometimes with an exactitude that borders on the absurd—the curriculum of a course. The existence of these standards is nothing new.

Take, for example, the subject I have taught for nine years: World History. The Department of Education for the state of California has an exquisitely detailed curriculum for this class. Never mind that I have profound misgivings about the focus of this course on the 20th Century to the detriment of antiquity, the Middle Ages, World Religions, The Renaissance, et cetera. I accept that I am merely an employee and that my employer has the right to tell me what to teach. The problem lies in the reality that this level of oversight has undermined the potential to create an extraordinary classroom atmosphere. In addition to stringent curricular standards, teachers are now given a variety of tools and commandments that sometimes include benchmark exams (exams that are given every few weeks to make sure that every teacher in a department reaches the same place in the course curriculum), pacing guides (suggestions about what pace to teach the curriculum), and state standard examinations (the climatic Holy Grail of modern education). Teachers are expected to use the same book, encouraged to give the same units tests and even the same final examination. In other words, there is a conscious effort to make

every classroom the same. We are all expected to literally
and figuratively be "on the same page." In such an arrange-
ment the identity of the teacher is incidental to the outcomes
of the course. In a word, education is to become "standard."

On its face, there is nothing particularly sinister or draconian about such instruments and practices. The standardization of education is, *prima facie*, a wholly benign practice.
After all, there are very good reasons why these practices
have become necessities in the minds of most school administrators. For too long the quality of a student's education
was contingent on sheer chance. Is it fair within a school for
one student to sit in a classroom that is interesting, exciting,
and informative while other students taking the same course
with a different teacher have to sit in a different classroom
that lacks all of the aforementioned virtues? More broadly, is
it fair in a public school system for many of the high-quality
teachers to gravitate to schools populated by middle and upper income students? Wasn't the dream of Horace Mann or
Thomas Jefferson to offer a quality education to all students
regardless of class, race, or neighborhood in the hopes of
bolstering an informed democracy?

What is possibly so pernicious about making sure that
all students can read at grade level and write with a high
degree of clarity and grammatical competence? What is possibly wrong with ensuring that every student, no matter their
natural proclivity or aversion to math, masters the basics of
mathematics, from arithmetic to algebra? How can we claim
to have a proficient education system if students cannot
recite the basics about their nation's history and government?
Anecdotal late-night television skits highlight with keen
humor the high degree of ignorance Americans have about
their own society. How can legislators and other policy-
makers be blamed for adopting a more pragmatic approach
to educational outcomes? The much-maligned No Child

Left Behind was clearly a response to those who believed that educational opportunities had become the privilege of those who live in more affluent neighborhoods. By setting universal standards and instituting a reward and punishment system for school performance in meeting these standards, there is a trickle-down effect that has drastically altered the landscape of the American classroom. From disproportionate attention on testing to a narrowing of the classroom curriculum, there is a chilling effect on a classroom when real and palpable punishments—from failing to win tenure to school-wide funding cuts—can be leveled against those teachers whose students do not perform well on standardized tests.

There is a strong disincentive in this new model to continue doing what great teachers do: teach deliberately. In the early days of my career I allowed my class to take an entire period to discuss an issue or concept they were genuinely interested in, even if there was no prospect of it appearing on a standardized test come April. The reason I revere teaching World History is because it is ripe with possibilities for interesting and substantive discussions—from the Fatalism of Sophocles in Ancient Greece to the modern realities of a rising China and India. It is difficult enough for a teacher to spark a genuine interest in mature intellectual matters. When such a spark is ignited, which usually occurs without planning or intent, it ought to be the obligation of a teacher to stoke it as much as possible. Unfortunately, in recent years, my classroom mantra has become, "Fascinating question, great comment, but we really need to move on." Instead of mastering the civilizations of Augustine's Rome, Elizabeth's England, or De Medici's Florence, we engage in peripheral lectures and activities that are likely to appear on a benchmark or state test.

What I fear is that the current method of outcome-based learning will become the new poster child for the lesson of unintended consequences. The reason why state governments and its leaders have had to assume a dogmatic posture towards the teaching profession is not because the majority of teachers are not professional in their behavior and dedicated in their manner. It is because of the deficient teachers who never followed the standards or the courses of study in the first place. The tragedy of the metamorphosis I have described is that it is more likely to transform and alter the teaching behavior of teachers who were already doing their jobs with a high degree of excellence.

Teachers who don't monitor the progress of their students or who pass out dittos endlessly or simply fail to explain concepts and content with a scintilla of clarity will still be poor teachers in this standardized environment. In fact, these teachers can feign excellence by teaching exclusively to the test. In my particular subject and in my particular state I could narrowly teach five topics the entire year—The Industrial Revolution, World War I, The Rise of Totalitarianism World War II, The Cold War—by redundantly drilling the same information day after day. It would be a terrible learning environment for the students. It would be a soul crushing migraine-inducing one-hundred eighty days of class. But their scores would probably show that they had mastered World History.

Such infantile thinking about the proper measuring stick for teaching outcomes propagates so many negative consequences, from encouraging redundant teaching methods to discouraging the best and the brightest from entering a public classroom, that it hardly merits a list.

In recent years the entire concept of a "social studies department" has become a relic of the past. Instead, departments have largely been replaced with smaller teacher groups known as professional learning communities (PLC's) that are grouped according to the subject matter. There are, for instance, two PLC's at my high school in the social studies department: one for World History and the other for US History. To say that I am fond of the people who populate my World History PLC is an understatement. They are smart, funny, and fabulously endearing people to be around. Their pride is infectious and they are evidence that teachers can, when encouraged, completely change the way they teach in order to be in compliance with the ever-changing expectations being placed upon them by everybody from the governor of California to their PLC leader, which happens to be me.

Lately, though, there is a quiet, almost completely unspoken sadness that rears its head at times; I can detect it from both the young teachers, who feel cheated of something essential in the teacher-student experience, and the veterans, who feel as though something profound has been lost in the midst of our OBE fervor. Their sadness has a narrative that goes something like this:

The state sets the curriculum, we teachers write tests that test the curriculum, then teach to the test. When students don't demonstrate enough mastery we teach and test again. And then teach and test some more. And...well, you get the idea. Modern educational researchers whose names become associated with the latest educational craze or pedagogic fad lend credence to our practices as we quote this author or that study and act as though we are part of the final stage of educational evolution, members of a capstone movement that is the culmination of the inherited wisdom of all thinking from the Ancient Greeks to the Stanford School of Education. These experts all seem to go out of their way to demonstrate that shorter and more frequent testing results in higher scores. So we write even more tests—more CFA's (common formative assessments) and less summative tests (longer tests at the end of a longer thematic unit that the dinosaurs used to use). We use high-tech programs to become more "data-driven teachers," disaggregating data to look at specific strands of curricular mastery and failure, we block out months of time to review the material for the Holy Grail state exams, we study the released questions and brainstorm about which topics we agree are likely candidates for the state exams. And then we review some more. When the exam results are released and we do well we deign ourselves as paragons of professionalism, masters of our epoch of education, patting each other on the back and telling each other that we are maestros of World History.

But then we take a step back and consider what we really achieved in the time we had with our students. We wonder how much they remember months after the exam is over. Most importantly, we wonder if our students love history any more than they did when they first entered our classrooms the previous fall. Everybody suddenly falls silent. We know that we did our jobs, as the public understands it. We know the numbers look good on paper. But we wonder if good numbers and the designations they breed—"proficient" and "advanced"—are genuine descriptions of the outcomes we've sown.

We aren't frauds, of course, but there are days and parts of the year when we are made to feel that way. It takes but a single learned quote from a teaching romantic who is clearly moved by the undertow of inspiration to make all of us feel small. On moments like these I am unfortunately reminded of Einstein's quote that, "Without creative personalities able to think and judge independently, the upward development of society is as unthinkable as the development of the individual personality without the nourishing soil of the community." By this measure, a fraud can produce good test scores but does very little to foster "creative personalities" in his students or the capacity to "judge independently." As one of my fellow teachers and best friends in all the world succinctly put it to me recently, "Maybe the generation we teach now will turn around in twenty-five years and condemn us for letting Petrarch and Voltaire and Lincoln fall out of standards, but we do what we are asked to do and then some."

If I am going to criticize this specific paradigm of teaching that has been thrust upon the modern educator, then I also possess an obligation to explain what is preferable. The root of the problem lies in the essence of what a standard is. The very ontology of something that is "standard" is essentially that it is ordinary. It is commonplace. Most legislators would affirm this observation with glee. "Absolutely," they would say, "basic knowledge of reading, writing, math, social studies, and science should be ordinary. It should be commonplace. The fact that it is extraordinary for students to possess mastery of these subjects is evidence that the system isn't working." In this view, if my students can regurgitate a few names, dates, and places on a multiple-choice exam they are deemed "proficient" or even "advanced." To believe that filling in bubbles on an answer document is the apogee of student achievement is as misguided as the child who believes Thanksgiving is about turkey or the Fourth of July exists only to light off colorful fireworks. I know that some students are good test takers, but can they tell me how the Greeks and the Romans understood the world through their own ancient eyes? Can my students explain the roots of modern science, the development of democracy or the transition from European mercantilism to industrial capitalism? Did they have time to read Erich Marie Remarque's *All Quiet on the Western Front* in order to truly grasp what it was like to live and fight in trenches during World War I? In short, did they use their time in World History to consider some of the more sweeping concerns of human life? If they did, then it is an experience and an education they will never forget. But the juggernaut that no one seems to have an answer to is how do we test this brand of instruction that is quickly becoming passé? How do we judge its merit and worth? What quick assessment can be given to discern if the teacher has done his job or not?

In the spring of my senior year of high school my enigmatic polymath of an English teacher decided it would be interesting if we took a week off from reading Shakespeare or Greek mythology to put on a student-written play. I think he noticed that we were getting burned out, that we were beginning to succumb to the pseudo-ailment of senioritis. So he adjusted; some of the students were actors, some collaborated to direct, others did publicity to advertize our extemporaneous efforts. It wasn't Broadway and no one's performance merited a Tony. We did it in the open air of the campus instead of on a stage. But there was a pleasure that accompanied the learning, a pleasure we all assumed was no longer accessible through a high school classroom that seemed to grow stale as the spring wore on. Our pleasure was derived from the fact that many of the things we had learned in the English class that year empowered us to put on the production. We weren't just learning literature, but we were bringing it to life. We made it organic.

More than the play itself, the process taught all of us an important lesson about the richness of education. Good teaching goes beyond the classroom. In fact, the only good teaching that matters is that which echoes beyond the classroom corridors.

When I think back on that wonderful episode of my life, I wonder if my English teacher would—or could—do such a thing today. Filling our students' heads with dry and detached data will serve them well on a test, but not in life. Educators are finding that they are no longer allowed to play

favorites with the subject matter they teach. An English
teacher who finds great delight in the short story or a history
instructor who glories in the twists and turns of The French
Revolution has to be careful nowadays. The era of the isolated teacher "doing his own thing" has become synonymous
with antiquarianism—so passé, so old school, so unsophisticated in a world where we now sit on a privileged perch
looking back at the glaring teacher errors of old. But when I
think back on the classes and the teachers that really made a
difference in my life, each one was *sui generis*, unique to the
point, perhaps, of eccentricity. Which makes me veer into
the realm of the heretical by asking: what is wrong with a
class in which a teacher takes a little extra time on a unit that
he or she finds especially interesting?

Different teachers have different specialties. I might
use the Enlightenment to capture the imaginations of my
students. Another teacher might specialize in the World
Wars. In such a situation, we will operate at a difference
pace; we will give different assignments; we will probably
give different assessments. In a word, we will each approach
these units in a decidedly non-standardized manner. But
the outcome of instilling a love for history remains constant. If teachers are to be anything other than curricular
automatons, then preserving at least a small iota of teacher
autonomy becomes essential. To cultivate a genuine love for
a subject can be accomplished in countless ways. But the one
way to ensure that learning is tantamount to boredom is to
make sure all teachers and classrooms are the same.

Let me be clear: standards are important. They should
exist and be energetically enforced by administrators and
states. Teachers who don't teach them should be reprimand-
ed. (Interestingly, and ironically, the same poor teachers
who brought on this new paradigm are the first ones to complain about losing their autonomy that allowed them to be

poor teachers in the first place). But standards should be the beginning of the classroom experience, a bare minimum, not a comprehensive end all be all. To standardize every facet of the learning experience is to deprive education of it enchanting potential to engender genuine intellectual curiosity and understanding. It is to incarcerate teachers into a zone of redundancy that robs the classroom of all that it can be. Good teachers will still be good teachers in a standardized teaching arena. But the arena will not be of their making.

Six years ago I began an Advanced Placement (AP) program at my high school—another form of standardized education—in American Government. This subject was what I entered the classroom to teach. I longed to teaching the students who wanted an intellectual challenge, longed to teach a subject that was my specialty, and was more than jubilant to be a pioneer for the class at my high school. AP tests have been around since I was in high school in the early 1990's and even earlier. There has never been any question that the curriculum for these courses revolve around the cumulative test given every May. The entire course is structured to maximize the chances for success on this examination. Students who pass the exam are usually given college credit for an introductory political science class and thus don't have to take it in college.

When I first taught AP classes six years ago, most students only took a handful of other AP courses concurrently with mine. English and Calculus are also popular AP courses on campus during senior year. What was genuinely interesting about my first few years of teaching AP is something that has now vanished. They naturally understood that there were overlapping ambitions. Yes, we studied American Government for a variety of benign reasons—to bolster civility, justify and question patriotism, cultivate convictions—but there was something exhilarating and magical about collectively preparing for the challenge of taking the AP test in May. It was reminiscent of a coach preparing his team for a competition. There was a strong spirit of camaraderie in the early years of teaching AP classes. Yes, they all wanted to pass the test for themselves. But there was also an element of school pride involved in our preparatory toils for the May exam. They would ask, "Mr. Adams, what's your goal? What kind of a passage rate would you be happy with?" There was nothing suspicious about my own desire to have a healthy and successful program as measured through the lens of a passage rate.

That's not to say I didn't have my caveats about AP curriculum. I did and still do. There is not enough time to really engage in current events. In some ways, the curriculum is so centered on the minutiae of government—congressional committees, behavior of the federal bureaucracy, a goliath body of court cases—that there was hardly any time to pay attention to a presidential or mid-term election going on around us, no time to discuss a war that had so evenly divided the country. Moreover, there was no time for me to take a few weeks and study some of the more important and interesting facets of politics, from my own perspective. To this day, I would like to take a week to teach them about the nuanced but extraordinary political thinking of Abraham Lincoln. I would like to take a few extra days at the beginning of the course and emphasize the reformulation of politics as conceived of by the founders of modernity which emphasized freedom and rights and compare it to the virtue-based political thinking of the classical world of the Greeks and Romans. I would like to have a mock confirmation hearing for the Supreme Court and do some class debates about current public policy questions. In other words, I wish I had the latitude to focus on some of the minutiae that I personally find interesting. But in the day and age of standardization, colleges across the country don't trust individual teachers to craft advanced curriculum on their own.

In the early days of teaching AP, the students instinctively understood that there was only so much time we could spend on each topic. In a certain sense, having the curriculum written by someone else gave me cover from the onslaught of complaints about having to know dozens of court cases or remember every single informal power of the president. But in the last two or three years something profound and frightening has begun to transpire in my AP classes. The year starts off well with positive attitudes and curious minds. But as the season for AP review begins around the beginning of April, attitudes and dispositions quickly begin to change. It isn't that seniors are ready to be done with high school and resent the workload, though they do get bored and lazy. Bored and lazy I can understand, but cynical and jaded I cannot. There is an adversarial air that some of the students begin to emit. They resent the notion of being forced to review for an exam they question the merit of.

"Why," they have recently begun to ask, "are we studying for an exam that really isn't a replacement for a college course? Shouldn't high school be high school and college be college? There is no way to truly duplicate the college experience when sitting in a high school class. We shouldn't fool ourselves."

Another common sentiment is that the review process casts a dyspeptic shadow on the entirety of the course. "When we were learning the material the first time," they comment, "it seemed like you wanted us to know and understand this stuff because it was important, because we should know it as citizens and as human beings. During the review we just feel like a cog in a testing machine...like you need us to validate your own program."

That one hurt. But not as much as the last major complaint.

"As long as there is a test at the end of the course that's all we're really going to care about. Taking the class is about being able to list it on college applications. Passing the test is just so we don't have to worry about government ever again."

It is important to note that this last sentiment is an amalgamation of different comments and conversations I have had over the past few years. I can't think of any student who would be that brazenly disrespectful (or honest). But it doesn't take a lot to read through their semi-polite protests. And this is definitely not the view of every student. Indeed, it is a minority opinion. What bothers me is that the minority is growing. As the pressure to take more and more AP classes grows, I have noticed that the students who take a ridiculous number of AP tests and classes tend to leave high school with a bitter taste in their mouths. For them, the waning days of high school are about regimented testing, not "learning for life" or any other high-minded aphorism. They know that teachers care about their students passing the AP exam and reflexively wager that that is all the teachers care about. Their academic grumpiness is spurred on by the evaporation of joy in the learning process as their high school careers grind to an end. A lachrymose army of AP students inching towards an anti-climatic graduation casts a disconcerting shadow on the waning weeks of my time with them.

What I find most interesting is that the students who only take one or two AP classes generally feel very differently. They react the way my students did the first few years I taught the course. "Bring on the AP," they think to themselves, "we can do it." They take the AP tests and feel vindicated for attempting to take a college level course for the first time, no matter if they pass the test or not. These students are also the types who need the review process and don't

resent a teacher who pushes them to excel on a standardized test. In the first few years of teaching AP courses, few
students took five or six AP tests a year. But that standard is
becoming increasingly common as the competition to win
acceptance to top schools has greatly accelerated. Gone are
the days of focusing on a few AP courses and trying to get
the most out of each one. We have created a college application culture where quantity has become confused with
quality.

It is apparent, then, that all students, at all levels, are
now on a steady intellectual diet of standardized education,
either from state governments, the federal government, or
from the writers of AP curriculum, the College Board. To
imagine educational policies continuing on their current trajectory leads one to imagine a teaching universe in the future
that was unimaginable just a generation ago.

To describe such a universe, let us engage in the following thought-experiment: imagine a time in the not-
so-distant future when a visionary policy maker in a state
legislature somewhere makes a daring suggestion in the face
of the following widely-accepted perceptions (not facts):
scores remain low throughout the state. There are still large
discrepancies between the achievements of wealthy schools
versus those schools further down the socio-economic scale.
The best teachers continue to flock to those campuses that
are already high achieving. The best students from the best
schools in America refuse to enter the teaching profession
because of the arduousness of the credentialing process, the
standardization of teaching once they get in the classroom,
and the stagnant pay were they to make a career of it. Billions upon billions of dollars continue to be poured into an
enterprise that doesn't appear to be working. State deficits
grow worse. Principals have no power over which teachers
to keep on staff. They can't fire anyone. There is no recourse

against teachers who, for whatever reason, fail to do their job well. Short of having a sexual relationship with a student, using profanity in every lecture, or using the school's chemistry lab to grow illegal narcotics, there is little the system can do to purge poor teachers. International comparisons grow bleaker. America seems to fall further and further behind. High-skilled jobs are being outsourced to India and Europe. Low-skilled jobs are going to China and Mexico. Our technological edge continues to atrophy. There is no Space Race but there is the economic rise of the EU, India, and China. Americans fret that America in not the hegemonic power it once was. America quickly begins to resemble the waning British Empire at the end of the 19th century or Constantine's Rome when it relocated to Constantinople in the 4th century to escape the encroachment of the barbarians.

In the face of so much social malaise and national despair, an innovation-minded policy maker in some state might stumble upon a panacea that combines desperation with the American love of innovation.

Abolish all teachers and replace them with a form of online learning!

The immediate reaction to this proposal is to scoff and label it an amalgamation of imagination, satire, and acute paranoia. But such a reaction is not warranted. A growing body of research suggests this may not be the stuff of science fiction or teacher paranoia. A key aspect of our economic dynamism since the dawn of the Industrial Era is to steadily replace human jobs with automation. Structural unemployment, i.e. unemployment caused by structural changes to the economy such as automation or out-sourcing, is a central feature of any vibrant economy, what Joseph Schumpeter might label "creative destruction." Teachers could just as easily join the ranks of horse and buggy drivers, bank tellers, and a laundry list of manufacturing jobs. The history books would note that in the early part of the 21st century the convergence of technology and demand for real equality of opportunity necessitated a radical break from teaching methods of the past.

This experimentation in education could begin as a pilot program in small districts throughout the state. If those districts, parents, and students were pleased with the outcomes then this pilot program could be augmented and encouraged on a district-by-district basis until it finally becomes the new method of operation in public education throughout the state. Of course, this new method of classroom instruction would also be phased in over the horizon of a student's education. A kindergarten student is not as capable of garnering the potential benefits of such a program as a freshman in high school.

In the status quo, when a state legislature creates education reform, it sometimes takes years for these reforms to trickle down and alter the teaching habits of teachers. The advantage of a computerized system is that problems are quickly solved, whether it is the quality of a lesson, the grade distribution on an exam, or even the content of the standards themselves. There is no waiting on teachers to change. Teachers, we all know, resist change and encroachment on classroom autonomy as though it were the Bubonic Plague. Centralization allows changes to be instituted virtually immediately.

Whatever state uses this model can serve as a beacon for other states. As Justice Louis D. Brandeis famously wrote in 1932, "It is one of the happy incidents of the federal system that a single courageous state may, if its citizens choose, serve as a laboratory; and try novel social and economic experiments without risk to the rest of the country." In short, the utility of American federalism is that it encourages innovation in the arena of policy making on a state-by-state basis. Wisconsin led the way in welfare reform in the 1990's. Massachusetts was a model for reforming America's health care system. No Child Left Behind was largely written by a Massachusetts senator, Ted Kennedy, but was inspired by the Texas school system of then-governor George W. Bush. These policies are not universally embraced and, in some instances, are highly controversial; and to a certain degree, that is precisely the point. They were all embryonic policy solutions at the state level that found a voice on the national public policy platform, buoyed by their perceived successes in their infancy.

Let us consider the positive externalities that would result from the implementation of such a radical policy:

1 Perfect standardization: The central complaint that some students receive a poor quality education through no fault of their own would be rendered moot. Every student across the state would receive the same lesson on roughly the same day with the same exercises. Student questions could be emailed to instructors who are sitting at a computer consul in the state's Department of Education answering questions by the thousands. All tests would be compiled from the same central test bank to ensure that all students take classes that are equally difficult or easy. Schools would have the flexibility to reschedule a class session if it wanted to schedule an all-school assembly, or if there is an unforeseen shutdown of the school or the computer network crashes. In the status quo, if a student misses a lecture or an activity he or she can't really make it up. The student might make up the homework or copy down the lecture notes, but the experience is qualitatively different than having sat through the class. In this new framework of education, the student is free to make up the lesson at a convenient time as long as all past lessons are presumably available on the computer network.

The vast potential for human error would be stamped out in a single stroke. Consider all the following common teacher errors that would be instantly eradicated:

- Teachers who fail to cover all of the material as laid out in the standards
- Teachers who spend too much time on one element of the curriculum and rush through the others
- Teachers who get sidetracked by engaging in conversations, which have no relevance or relationship to the material that is supposed to be taught
- Teachers who are too funny
- Teachers who are too dull
- Teachers who make inappropriate comments
- Teacher who want to talk about sports or current events instead of the curriculum
- Teachers who play favorites
- Teachers who don't grade and refuse to turn back work
- Teachers who rely too much on films and dittos
- Teachers who just can't teach

I would like to think that teachers teach for the most noble of reasons. I would like to think they share my ambitions for the classroom and my romanticism about the enchantment of learning. This is folly, of course. On the very first day of my teacher credentialing classes ten years ago, the Education professor made every student introduce him or herself, tell which subject we aspired to teach, and finally, explain why we decided to become teachers. The standard answers were given.

"I want to make a difference."

"I love my subject."

 "I love children."

There was one middle-aged man who slouched comfortably in his desk at the back of the classroom. I'll never forget the wry smile on his face. When his turn to render his justification for becoming a teacher came he slowly sat up in the desk and said, "I'm honest unlike everyone else in here. I have three reasons, not one, for becoming a teacher: June, July, and August." Everyone giggled and the professor looked as annoyed as you can look on the first day of a class. No one doubts that there are teachers of this ilk at every school in America.

2 Real equality of opportunity: Americans are quick to note that they believe in "equality of opportunity, not equality of condition." This is a nice turn of phrase, but upon closer scrutiny—even as an ideal—it is relatively untenable. Some Americans have large advantages over others on the road to success. Instead of equalizing the playing field for all members of the socio-economic strata, more often that not our educational system perpetuates the gap in real opportunity by providing unequal educational opportunities to different slices of America's social fabric. If there is the potential for a great equalizer in a society that honors liberty and self-reliance, it is surely education. Since the time of Horace Mann, Americans have held education as one of the most sacrosanct rights enjoyed by all citizens. Government cannot change the quality of parents a child receives. Government cannot alter the fact that some students are gifted—academically, athletically, artistically—while others simply are not. Government cannot nullify every episode of bad fortune in the life of its citizens. But what government can do is provide the same education to every student. I don't know a single American who would argue that some children deserve a qualitatively better education than others. Americans of conscience and conviction can disagree about tax rates, wars, and energy policy. But providing every child

with a high quality education is a bridge in a divided country.

Liberals argue that the poor performance of urban schools has two main culprits: a lower property tax base and quality teachers migrating to affluent campuses. These structural deficiencies translate into fewer resources, fewer opportunities, and thus lower performance. Conservatives argue that it is a matter of values and behavior. Where there is a lack of parental support, there will also be a lack of successful educational outcomes. No amount of funding or reform will alter this. A conservative, who is not a politician, might rightly say, "If you want better schools, be better parents." No teacher, school or standard can take the place of a home in which parents read to children, help with homework, instill a college-going mentality from the time children are young, and make no excuses when the student ditches class, fails a test, or decides to stop doing homework.

Most sensible Americans know that there is truth in both of these claims. The elimination of teachers and the institution of truly standardized education would level the playing field to such an extent that, as long as high quality remains, both sides would have something to gain. Liberals could no longer complain that poor students receive less classroom opportunity than the more affluent students. Conservatives could argue, once and for all, that if scores among schools don't change then there are social factors that have to be addressed outside the classroom.

3 Huge financial savings for states: The state of California spends roughly fifty-six billion dollars a year on education. Most advocates of public education argue that this is a small price to pay for the economic and political benefits of having an educated citizenry. Still, in an era of large national and state budget deficits, leaving the next generation

of Californians and Americans saddled in debt and addicted
to structural government deficits is deeply injurious to their
prospects for a bright future. The change I am proposing
could, in a single stroke, change deficits into surpluses.

To staff a large high school with over one hundred
highly trained teachers, secretarial and custodial support
staff, as well as teacher aides and security, is a very expen-
sive enterprise. A new education system that is completely
computer and digitally oriented would only require a skeletal
staff on campus. Classrooms would be quickly converted to
computer labs. More than thirty students could sit in each
computer lab. A professional who is a hybrid of a computer
tech, security guard, and operational manager would monitor each room. This professional would collect and grade
homework and input the scores into a state-centered grading system. This person would also be in charge of taking
attendance, monitoring class behavior, and ensuring that all
students are on-task. Computer knowledge, classroom man-
agement skills, and grading according to a rubric are all skills
that would be required in this new position. A bachelor's
degree would no longer be required since this person is only
a classroom facilitator, not a teacher. The actual teaching
will be accomplished at the computer consul. The teaching
credential would also be unnecessary. A simple classroom
certificate or junior college education would be enough to
equip an individual with the skills to monitor the classroom.
As a result of requiring fewer skills, less education, and having larger classes, the amount of money devoted to classroom instruction would be drastically reduced.

The amount of money that is saved from teacher sala-
ries would empower the state to put massive resources into
the development of the online curriculum. The primary
argument against computerizing education is that it will lack
the human touch as students become easily bored and grow

disinterested. However, instead of being taught by the same teacher every day, students would encounter a cornucopia of different teaching modalities at their service. Some days they might watch a lecture from an expert in the field they are learning about. Some days there would be an exercise or activity to complete on-line. Examinations are done on-line. Students sitting next to each other might have slightly different tests to minimize the chances of cheating.

The savings and economic benefits garnered from the automation of public education would be immense. There is a benefit to everyone no matter your political orientation. Taxes could be cut. Funds for new education programs that offer additional tutoring or field trips or other enrichment activities would be plentiful. New universities would be constructed. College tuition costs would finally go down, not up, as college would become more affordable and accessible to all of a state's high school graduates. The deficits that annually materialize in my home state of California— almost twenty billion dollars this year—would be a relic of the past; assuming legislators don't ambitiously redirect the old money from education into a new entitlement or government program. State debt could be quickly paid off and tomorrow's citizens would be left with a desirable fiscal situation—low taxes, a well-educated workforce—from which to build a promising economic future. In such an environment, businesses would flock to the state en masse to take advantage of its labor and tax policies. As it now stands, the next generation of Americans will be burdened with a life of higher taxes and less of a safety net than the current generation. Today's spending bonanzas at the national and state level are financed largely through the structural deficits that will have to be paid back by Americans who are barely out of the crib. And while this education reform is not a cure to the national unfunded liabilities in Social Security and Medicare, it is a first step towards fiscal responsibility on a state level.

4 Former teachers enter different industries: Perhaps some former teachers will elect to stay in the classroom in the lesser role I have already described. In the short run, there is no question that putting teachers out of work will wreak havoc on thousands of families—that is why teachers would slowly be fazed out over time. Most teachers would have years to realize that they should seek a new career. In the long run, the infusion of efficient and educated labor into different industries would be a boom for the economy. Teachers who do not believe in the paradigm shift to online learning are free to open up charter schools using old methods of teaching. Perhaps some will open up private schools in the spirit of entrepreneurship and make more money than they ever did in the public sector. Many other teachers would go back to school once more to receive more education and enhance their skill set in order to be more valuable in the labor market.

5 Colleges already have online classes and distant learning: There are a variety of technological tools that now allow colleges to teach courses without the student and teacher ever being in the same classroom. Virtual classrooms, collaborative software, and distance learning are now tools that are frequently employed in universities across America to allow students to learn online. The proliferation of online learning at the collegiate level could be easily adapted to suit the standardization requirements of states across the country. It is important to note that teaching will not become obsolete. What will become obsolete is having the same teacher who teaches the same subject to the same set of students every single day of a school year. This old way of looking at the ideal student setting is the root of the problem

in education.

This tongue-in-cheek thought-experiment of glimpsing into a possible scenario of the future is not as far-fetched as one might imagine. It is a future, of course, that I passionately reject! What I have just elucidated in painstaking detail is a future that is concomitant with the current obsession with standardized education. These are the arguments that might be used. The problem is that no matter how many positive social and political impacts one can derive from replacing human teachers with automation via computers, the classroom will never achieve its highest possibilities if we forget that, besides parenting, education is the most human of human activities.

A computer can demonstrate an idea, but it cannot make it inspirational. A computer can provide mountains of information, but it cannot articulate why it's important to master. Even if the lessons on the computer are of the highest quality, it is difficult to be inspired or acquiesce to the importance of a subject if the hallmark of a standardized classroom is depersonalization. Online learning will rarely make a student laugh or think. Distance learning won't ask a student why he or she looks sad. A computer program cannot evoke a community of learning in which every student feels connected to another human being who is older and concerned with the well-being of the students. Learning, like love, friendship, or faith, should be intensely personal.

This begs the central educational question of our time: Is teaching a science or an art?

This is the fundamental schism between advocates of a truly universalized education of standards versus those old pedagogic fuddy-duddies like myself who believe that the moment education becomes impersonal for students it loses both its magic and its utility. Those who want to standardize not merely the curriculum (which I have no qualms with), but also the teachers in the classroom who teach that curriculum, are clearly apostles of the teaching-is-a-science philosophy of learning. In their view, teaching is akin to the scientific method: follow the same standards, don't allow subjective tastes or personality traits to interfere, and follow the same steps in every single classroom, every single day, with every single subject.

It is the scientist who attempts to provide an objective understanding of the world. It is the artist who tells us how this objective world should affect our subjective minds. Or to state my case even more radically, it is the artist who changes the nature of our subjective mind—and in so doing—alters the reality of the objective world.

Teachers can still be practitioners of standards but simultaneously artists of human transformation. Art often portrays scientific knowledge in an artistic structure. The rationalism of the Enlightenment is artfully captured in the symmetrical music of Mozart or the prose of Ibsen. The cosmic relativism as discovered by Einstein is clearly reflected in the shattering of artistic standards by Joyce and Picasso. Likewise, teachers can teach standards but adapt those standards to their own individual strengths and methods.

The truth is that there is no single solution, no panacea, for all of the ailments that plague the modern American classroom. Perfect standardization robs the classroom of any artistry. No standardization, on the other hand, results in egregious gaps in educational opportunities. Even the best teachers will not reach and educate every child. Not everyone likes the same artists—some like Rembrandt, others favor Picasso.

But artists will never enter the classroom if their canvasses are completely beyond their control. The best teachers are on a constant search for that perfect mélange of classroom magic, from the formation of the desks to the content of their lessons. It is the height of arrogance to assume that there is a one-size-fits-all approach to educating today's children. In fact, just the opposite is required: constant adjustment and experimentation. But such adjustments require a measure of freedom. In his essay, "Of Eloquence," David Hume once observed, "We are satisfied with our mediocrity, because we have had no experience of any thing better."

Contact with the classroom is supposed to save each child from such a cynical proposition. Not every child will travel to Europe or partake in the splendors of attending world-renowned symphonies or walk through art exhibits. Instead, many are only given a simple classroom and a single teacher. It is only when genius is treasured and explored, beauty is demonstrated and exposed, and elegance of the mind is the ultimate goal of every classroom in America, that we can safely suggest that we have standardized the most important facet of the educational experience: the extraordinary.

CHAPTER V
ZOMBIES & ZEALOTS

We didn't know why he was acting odd.

Was it the fact that this was the last class he would ever teach before retiring? Was his wife's recent death from cancer the culprit of his oddities? Whatever the cause, I was never bored sitting in his class.

"I hate talking to people on airplanes, I hate it," Professor Martin would exclaim, speaking as though he were in the middle of telling a truncated joke. "Everybody wants to talk to you when they learn you're a philosophy professor."

He told the story of a conversation he recently had with a dental hygienist. He was in the dentist's chair and wasn't making eye contact. When he fatefully told her what he did for a living she cordially asked, "Well, what exactly does a philosophy professor do?"

Without missing a beat he turned around and looked her square in the face before spookily saying, "Oh, we sit around asking questions like 'is the reason I can't see my eyes the same reason why I can't see the back of my head?'"

"She didn't want to talk too much after that," he proudly said.

This was an introductory philosophy course. Professor Martin had probably taught this same course dozens of times throughout his long teaching career. There were a variety of signs that he was on the verge of retirement. One of my best friends also taking the course with me claims to have seen a copy of his doctoral dissertation sitting in a trashcan outside his office. The two of us kept waiting to see some trace of a heavy and downtrodden heart from this odd man. Maybe, we wagered, he would acknowledge that it was his last class. Maybe he would tear up at some point. Instead, we were treated to a barrage of oddball comments and behavior, some funny as hell, others that were deeply unsettling.

Examples? There were many…

He would casually—almost to the point of cold objectification—mention that his wife had recently died of cancer. He would give outlandish justifications for the grades he handed out. One of the girls in the class asked him why she received a "B" instead of an "A" on a short paper she had written. He looked at her with all the seriousness of life and death and glibly said, "I don't know. When I saw the paper it just screamed out 'B.' If I read it again maybe it would scream out 'A' or 'C.' That's all I got!"

The class's curriculum centered on the basic epistemological questions of the Western philosophic tradition. He did an extraordinary job explaining the basic tension between rationalism versus empiricism. What is the nature of knowledge: do we know something because we think it or because we perceive it? We diligently read our Descartes (*Cogito Ergo Sum*) and our Berkeley (*Esse est percipi*), hoping to clarify our thinking about the limitations and possibilities of human knowledge. He was the pinnacle of relaxed in class. He rarely stood up to write anything on the board and I distinctly remember him leaning back in his chair on more than one occasion.

This was a spring term course, which meant most students were not in an academic mindset. In my day, Washington & Lee had a non-orthodox academic schedule. Instead of embracing a quarter system of three ten-week quarters or a semester system of two fifteen-week semesters, W&L had an academic schedule that was a hybrid of the two. We had two twelve-week quarters and one six-week quarter in the spring.

Most students try to take a single class in the spring, leaving mountains of time for activities of a decidedly non-academic nature. The Shenandoah Valley in the beginning of the spring is about the closest thing to Eden on Earth. It doesn't surprise me that some students decided to use the opportunity to lounge in the sun, go hiking in the afternoons, drink away the evenings or take extended weekend road trips. But the consequence of such revelry is a lack of classroom verve and focus. Professor Martin was keenly aware of the Dionysian emphasis of his students. This was nothing new at W&L. For better or for worse, that was one of the quirks of the place. What probably bothered him was that this extracurricular focus became mutually exclusive with the necessary intellectual seriousness he demanded for the three hours a week he spent with us.

He would dramatically ask for questions, "So, are there any thoughts on the reading? Anything you need clarified? Any questions, at least?"

Silence would reign. The awkwardness didn't seem to bother him because he would keep scanning the room for hands.

"Anyone?"

He didn't raise his voice. In hindsight, I now realize that there is nothing more maddening for a teacher than to teach a class on a topic of extreme importance only to realize that the only person who seems to understand its importance is the teacher himself. I usually succumb to temptation and make a snide comment or let the students know my displeasure in other ways. But not Professor Martin. He would coolly say, "OK, fine. See you next time."

My friend and I were eager for the last class session of the quarter, not because we didn't enjoy the class, because we did. There were more mind-bending, jabberwocky-like questions in this class than I had ever heard before. Professor Martin had us questioning the basic assumptions of being a sentient, living being.

Can we ever overcome a subjective perspective of something in order to objectively know it?

How do we know our bed is where we left it this morning?

Do we project our own mental prejudices into our perceptions of the spatio-temporal world?

What we were eagerly anticipating was the scene of his last class. Surely, we hoped, he would have something splendid and grandiose to pronounce, perhaps one last denouement that would serve as a capstone to a long and distinguished teaching career. When the last day of class arrived, nothing stood out until the very end. My friend and I glanced at each other in anticipation.

"Any closing questions?" the professor innocently asked.

"Anything? About the material? About your final exam? Really....nothing?"

He leaned back in his chair and loudly proclaimed, "I am disappointed by the diffidence in this classroom." He just sat there in a posture that amounted to an exclamation point. Finally, he stood up and walked out the door. No one else seemed to feel the weight of the occasion. Everyone gathered up their belongings, shuffled it into their backpacks, and emptied out of the classroom for the final time. This was the last class in the last course the man would ever teach and he ended it with, "I am disappointed by the diffidence in this classroom."

At the time I felt bad for him. But what in the world did he expect of us? Either we understood the material or we didn't. Asking extraneous questions seemed more than a little bit pointless.

I never thought that ten years later—in the middle of my own teaching career—I would find a kindred soul in the memory of Professor Martin.

I have more in common with Professor Martin than I care to admit. It took me a few years to finally identify and accept what we have in common. It began with the faint throb of sadness at the end of every school year. At first, I thought this sadness was merely the residue of watching my students move on to a new stage of life as I stay ossified in the same classroom year after year. In some cases, I have known these students for four years. Isn't it natural for me to feel at least a patina of regret about their sudden departure from my life?

But my sadness is more than a heavy heart. I began to notice a few years ago a certain unsavory quality in the disposition of my departing seniors. In addition to the normal storms of senioritis and AP burnout, there was an ineffable attitude I had trouble identifying and explaining until recently. It's not that my students are unkind towards me or unappreciative of the education the faculty and I have attempted to provide for them. What they possess is the same malady of the classroom that Professor Martin identified in his last class. There is a certain diffidence that I, too, sense in my departing seniors. I would phrase it another way, however. What I have discovered is their subtle though potent belief that education and ideas are incidental to their happiness.

Looking back on the past few years of my career, this quiet but very real undercurrent of diffidence has always been there. But it was a conversation—the most consequential and traumatic I have ever had with a student—that made me open my eyes to see what has, perhaps, always been there. This student was one of the most brilliant young men I have ever encountered. I have no doubt that he will achieve great things in his life. His scores—GPA, SAT, AP—were each as close to perfect as one could hope for. His transcript was perfect and his activities were plentiful. He was every college committee's dream applicant.

Unfortunately, he also happens to be the singularly most maddening student I have ever encountered. I didn't realize this, however, until late into our relationship.

I have been fortunate in my career to teach three or four students who teeter on the border of genius. Their intellect soars over everyone else in the classroom. I know that I, perhaps, taught them new information, but it surely wasn't anything they couldn't have easily mastered on their own. It would not be hyperbole for me to admit that I wouldn't be surprised if one of them discovered a cure for cancer, sat on the Supreme Court, or wrote the great American novel of the 21st Century. What these students had in common was extraordinary humility about their talents and abilities. It is almost as if their genius transports them to a higher peak of human intelligence, a peak so high that they alone have the perspective of how high the mountain actually ascends. They look up from their vantage point and see the splendors of a world none of us can even imagine, let alone see from our much lower cognitive plateau. Perhaps this is why genius is sometimes synonymous with solitude. People like Beethoven, Schopenhauer, and Rousseau live and frolic in a mental cosmos that no one around them can relate to. The few students I have taught who experience life through the prism of genius seem to be genuinely humbled by what they see.

But there was not a trace of humility in this young man. I really wanted to like him. I tried and tried and tried to connect. But nothing in class was ever particularly interesting to him. He never seemed impressed by anybody or anything else. I would give him some outside readings to try to challenge him on a different level. When I asked him what he thought about the articles he would shrug and act as if it was nothing new to him. He had a mind as powerful as the other student-geniuses I have encountered, but he wasn't ascending to any peaks of wonderment.

We ran into each other in the hallway late in the spring, just a few weeks before his impending graduation. I was on my way to the office; we engaged in small talk for a moment before things got quickly—and very unexpectedly—personal. I still have no idea what conversational digression prompted his outburst.

"You're afraid of everything Mr. Adams," he said, uncomfortably close to my face. "I mean look at your life. Everything is safe: your job, your relationships. Everything is safe. It's kind of sad."

One of his friends, also a student of mine that I was rather fond of, just stood there leaning against the hallway wall, slowly stepping away from the volcanic conversation while shaking his head in horrified confusion. I looked over at him for comfort. He quietly uttered, "I don't know where all this is coming from. I have no part in it." But that didn't stop this young man from furthering his verbal assault on me.

"Life should be about new experiences," he confidently asserted. "There is so much to do in the world and you don't do any of it."

Part of me wanted to defend myself. Part of me wanted to obliterate his axiomatic and sophomoric world-view. But most of all, I wanted to use his own criteria against him to explain what an arrogant hypocrite he was. A student had never addressed me in such a brazen and personal manner before. It is essential to note that I pride myself on getting along with my students. I don't have personal confrontations in class. I have written one referral during my career. In a decade of teaching, I have never had an adversarial parent-teacher conference. The audacity of this young man was unparalleled in all my years as a student and as a teacher.

At first, my reaction was basic and expected. Quite simply, my feelings were severely hurt. I had never done anything but extend a hand of encouragement and hope to this young man. I had written him a recommendation letter earlier in the year before he took on a different and more menacing persona. I had helped him with an essay for a writing competition just a few weeks earlier. I had given him outside readings. I did all that I could do to be a decent mentor and teacher to him.

And yet, this was his opinion of me.

As the raw feelings of hurt eventually wore off, what remains of the confrontation is something more unsettling but worthy of my consideration. I painfully wondered how many students sat in my classroom, year after year, thinking the same thoughts. How many of my students harbor such a low opinion about the simple aspirations of a classroom teacher? I put myself in his shoes and what I saw of myself literally brought me to tears. This young man looked at me and saw a pathetic life filled with the opposite of what he valued. It is new experience he wanted, not monotony. Death is tantamount to redundancy. A classroom is not liberating. It is not a portal to wonderment. It is the most self-limiting of venues for young people who want nothing more than to break the very bonds I had placed on them. I have nothing to teach because I am, at my core, a peddler of passé teachings and phony platitudes.

The more I considered his perspective in the weeks following the incident, the more helpless I became. Every teaching virtue I thought I had slowly morphed into a vice. My enthusiasm only befits the fool. My love of the subject I teach assumes the glint of the ridiculous. At least a court jester knows in his heart that he exists only to amuse; he doesn't have the temerity to take himself too seriously. From this young man's perspective, my problem is that I don't know my rightful place in the lives of my students. What he was really saying was, "You're only a high school teacher. That fact alone merits my antipathy towards you. Only people who act on a grand stage and win grand achievement merit my respect. Only those who have the courage to venture beyond the classroom can live truly majestic lives. Stop trying so hard because I see through your smoke screen, Mr. Adams. All of the work, the energy, the pretense of actually having something to teach us, all of it is a giant farce. That is what my piercing intellect has allowed me to understand. You can fool others with your bravado; your theatrical, fancy quotes and elevated vocabulary. But you can't fool me. At your core, sir, you have no credibility. You're just a bullshit artist."

I wanted to tell him that one day someone he loved was going to unexpectedly die. I wanted to tell him that someday he was going to question his own greatness. I wanted to tell him that in all likelihood he will have his heart broken and that all his brilliance, all the power of that splendid brain in his cranium, wouldn't do a damn thing to make him a better person, a more loyal friend, or win back the love he's lost. I wanted to tell him that he doesn't have all the answers because he doesn't even know the important questions. I wanted to tell him that maybe tomorrow, maybe next week, or maybe in thirty years he is going to remember this conversation and shudder in shame at his behavior. Maybe he'll begin to see me a little closer to the way I see myself: a far from perfect teacher who is an even further from perfect human being. But for all my foibles and failures, I never had anything in my heart except hope for this young man. I wanted to help him get a glimpse of a future self that was shaped by the magic of the classroom. But such a glimpse is impossible for he who refuses to stand in awe of anything beyond himself.

This young man had in mind a peculiar species of hero, one that is part adventurer, part drifter. In such a shallow view of life's possibilities, there is no room for the saint or the poet, the father or the teacher. My constant advice to "find the extraordinary in the ordinary" is just a clever but ultimately empty turn of phrase. To this young man the extraordinary is the extraordinary. The ordinary is the ordinary. The domestic life of a high school teacher with three kids, a wife, and a mortgage can never be packaged as "extraordinary." To him, I wallowed in the ordinary out of fear, not because I find splendors of grandeur in a conventional life.

My lack of credibility in his eyes would never allow me to teach him something that I only know because of age and experience. He would mentally roll his eyes if I tried to tell him about the form of love I discovered when I met my wife. The complete and incomprehensible joy I found when becoming a father represents nothing but redundant obligation to him. And spending my days with young people in the same classroom teaching the same subject year after year while receiving a public employee's wage is not noble, it's simply sad. Nothing can be done to bridge the chasm between us. The hurt initially caused by this conversation has been replaced by sadness. In the time that has passed

since he graduated, I still don't know what I could have done
to teach him anything. I hope that college does for him what
I couldn't do. Maybe, in his eyes, college professors have
credibility. Maybe he'll be humbled the way I was when I
came into contact with people who knew more and had accomplished more than I had.

On a more complicated level, this confrontation illuminated with utter clarity the competing agendas within
a single classroom. Isaiah Berlin's concept of positive and
negative freedom perfectly demonstrates the differences that
often emerge between the teacher and his students. Negative
freedom allows an individual to act as she chooses because
of a lack of barriers or obstacles. In other words, individuals can act because nothing is standing in the way. Positive
freedom, on the other hand, allows an individual to act as
she chooses because of the presence of some characteristic or talent that allows the individual to achieve a desired
outcome. In the first instance, an individual is free to play
tennis because the gates are unlocked. In the second, the
individual can play tennis because she is in possession of the
skills that empower her to play the game. To attain an ideal
end both freedoms must be present.

The only thing this young man wanted, however, was
negative freedom. He wanted everyone—especially me, it
seemed—to just get the hell out of his way. Let him climb
mountains and go on safaris. Let him think what he wants
without mounting a challenge to it. This is precisely the
type of student who would have walked past Socrates on
the streets of Athens, the type who doesn't want to be tethered to an uncomfortable barrage of questioning. He would
rather stay in the Platonic cave looking at shadows as long as
they were his shadows, not someone else's. His intellectual
proclivity is to demystify, deconstruct, and discredit. Instead
of defending or refining a personal conviction, it is easier to

eviscerate others' instead.

But good teachers want something entirely different. To be human is to think, to desire, to act. Only zombies are indifferent about what we should think, how we should act, and how much we should desire. What we want to facilitate is positive freedom. Positive freedom has a communal and political component to it. It assumes that for students to do with their lives what they choose there are certain powers, passions, and knowledge they must possess. That is where the classroom comes in. This young man may want to be a doctor. There is literally nothing standing in his way. But he won't be able to do it without the study skills that are required for successful academic outcomes. He won't be able to do it without the knowledge teachers and books provide. He won't be able to do it without other doctors constantly critiquing him and telling him how to improve. In a word, he needs a community of learning and teaching to become the man he wants to become.

I actually have a great deal of faith that this young man will become a very different person than the one I found so arrogant and alienating. For there is a greater teacher this young man is sure to encounter that is stronger and louder than any book or professor he will ever meet: life. Life has a funny way of teaching us what we need to know. It teaches us, at different times and on different paths, that we all need other human beings. It teaches us that we need to grow and change to become the people we want to be. Most people eventually discover that being zombies of apathy or zealots of indifference is a fast path to despair. Once this young man learns this lesson he will possess the one thing that is necessary for genuine intellectual and moral growth: humility. Perhaps he will then devote himself not just to acting, but knowing why some actions are preferable to others. Perhaps he won't just believe something, but he will know why he believes it. Perhaps he will associate elegance with more than just the trappings of luxury and travel. Life will teach him if he listens.

I should probably go easy on the young man. After all, what offended and hurt me was not the content of his diatribe, but its aggressive and deeply personal method of delivery. But the content itself—that the classroom lacks the verve to lay the foundations for a meaningful and interesting life—is not particularly different from a message delivered by an entire cadre of valedictorians a few years earlier at the school's graduation ceremony. I remember feeling gently rebuffed by a group of students I thought the world of.

"The classes and teachers were fine," they all concluded with great aplomb, "but it was the fixtures of life outside the classroom that really make a difference." Each of them said it differently. Some were more explicit than others. But they all treated their teachers and the classroom as watered-down, second-tier influences. My drive home that evening was not nearly as joyful as it had been in years past. I tried to rationalize and understand what they were saying. Of course, I understood that friendships are a decisive facet in young people's lives. Of course, all the extracurricular activities are the context for the memories they will take with them for a lifetime.

How could I possibly begrudge them their opinion? Teenagers are social creatures. They experience the whirl-wind of high school through the collective ethos of a keen and sensitive social awareness. It is only when looking back on these years, usually in the sanitized safety of one's twenties or thirties, that they can fully separate themselves from the high school herd, to see these years for what they were, for better or for worse.

Or maybe I am just talking myself down from the proverbial ledge. Maybe it has taken me half a decade to see what has always been in front of me. Maybe I should thank this young man for being a pioneer, for acting as a modern-day Galileo, for having the guts to say what everyone has always thought but never had the nerve to say out loud, much less to my face.

His problem, and that of a great many of my students, is not that they suffer from a lack of opinions, per se. They have opinions on a wide variety of issues. It's just that they often seem unwilling to refine, strengthen, or reshape these opinions based upon anything they learn in the classroom. This represents a different, and perhaps more lethal, form of intellectual apathy. It is more than shrugged shoulders and stealth texting in the middle of class. It is an apathy that is wholly indifferent to some of the great questions all citizens of all persuasions should consider:

What is the greater good: peace or justice?

Should we be Jeffersonians or Hamiltonians in our political thinking?

Are there absolute transcendent values that we should aspire to know and live up to or is the moral universe only knowable through relative and shifting perspectives?

What is the proper balance between individual rights and civic duty?

But no matter the importance of the question or the vivacity of the class, I often get the same response: droopy eyes and disinterested shrugs. The education they receive neither bolsters their beliefs nor challenges them. Just like Professor Martin, I sense a certain diffidence in my students. This wouldn't bother me if there weren't so much at stake. My students happily bring their life experiences into the classroom. They just don't know what to do with them.

Pascal taught that human beings know too much to be skeptics but not enough to be dogmatists. The irony my students unknowingly demonstrate is that the only thing they are dogmatic about is their skepticism. To fully demonstrate the extent to which modern students believe education is purely an exercise in naked expediency, I note two very different reactions to the material being taught in my classroom: either they are zombies of indifference (shrugs, blank stares, stealth text messaging to God-knows-who as if I don't know they're doing it) or zealots of self-righteousness (don't ask me what I think, don't change my mind, just tell me what to know for the exam). To take an idea too seriously is the mark of the unsophisticated. To actually believe that a novel, a lecture, or a discussion might be decisive for a student's life is the pinnacle of the absurd. Such beliefs—to most students—are in the league of Santa Claus, Tinker Bell, or Mr. Snuffleupagus. More times than I care to admit I come face to face with a wall of students who believe that wisdom is cynicism recast as dispassion. Or worse yet, an ocean of knowing glances between the students that belie their common faith in the absurdity of their teacher's passion. I can only imagine what they're thinking:

"Who does this guy think he is? I wish he would drink some hemlock."

"Just tell us what we need to know."

"Don't try to change us. Leave me alone."

What we as teachers are trying to do is not to give answers—what to do, where to go, whom to marry—only to make sure that when the time does come for our students to answer such questions, they reach beyond the quotidian equations of their everyday lives. A life of substance requires a distinction between decisions of definition (Is God real? What do I want to be? Are moral claims absolute or relative?) versus decisions of the banal (where should I go on spring break?). The latter only requires a sense of taste and preference, the former an acknowledgement that some decisions are worth the worry and hesitation. My peculiar sadness is testimony to what happens when such a distinction isn't made at all. Shouldn't what we read in books and learn in the classroom figure into these decisions of definition?

I always assumed that they did. But I have begun to wonder lately. I am always tempted to go to the front of my classroom and write two quotes on the whiteboard, forcing them to embrace and defend one against the other:

Quote One: "There is only one inborn error, and that is the notion that we exist to be happy...So long as we persist in this inborn error...the world seems to us full of contradictions."

Quote Two: "Don't worry, be happy now!"

Never mind that one is Arthur Schopenhauer and the other is Bobby McFerrin—two very different seers of wisdom. What bothers me is that if I had to ask the lot of them to choose between these two divergent world-views of what it means to be alive, to be human, to inhabit a place in this world, many of them would consider the exercise to be perfectly pointless.

Why worry? Why think about it at all? The fact that there's no consensus must mean there's no correct answer. Right? Why invest oneself too much in anything, much less a cause whose certainty is as fluid as this one. Or even more radically, they might say that whatever you believe is your truth. In this solipsistic view, no one can ever venture beyond a subjective perspective.

Why argue?

Which brings me back to my hero. One of the reasons I cherish and promote the pedagogy of Socrates is his understanding that questioning and awe sit at the cradle of genuine knowledge and conviction. We ask, *then* we know. But with

a great many students, a radicalized form of intellectual in-
dividualism has crept its way into their classroom demeanor.
The question they ask themselves is not "how should I live"
or "what should I think," but instead, does this author or
politician or artist agree with what I already think? The educational process has been inverted from being an inductive
exercise of self-examination to a mentally hedonistic deduc-
tion of self-aggrandizement.

The difference is not subtle! Do we read Emerson, or
study Jefferson, or listen to Wagner simply to find a like
mind, to find authority behind what we, ourselves, already
think? If so, education merely becomes a cerebral potpourri
of ideas and tastes—some we accept, some we reject, without
ever exploring the rudimentary reasons for doing so. Not
only does this propagate a morally relative universe in which
perspective trumps objectivity, but it also diminishes the
utility of engaging in the free interplay of ideas. What good
can come of a discussion when none of the participants are
willing to concede or re-examine anything?

One is left to wonder if this is the beginning of a new
brand of 21st century sophistication. Perhaps I am presiding
over the advent of some archetype-shattering shift in student
attitudes and behavior. Old sophistication is akin to a charis-
matic worldliness: read, think, discuss, and acquire a decent
understanding of the world. This takes time, intelligence,
and yes, even a small smattering of hard work—think James
Bond before he entered MI6.

But this is Old World thinking. New sophistication is
the embodiment of something entirely different and without precedent. This new pseudo-sophistication swathes
my students in a mental cocoon within which nobody need
intrude. They are warm and comfortable, ever confident that
the future will be full of more freedom, more wealth, and
more progress than before. (Aren't they curious about how

they became so free and so wealthy?) This is a sophistication that has faith in history's singularity of direction. There is no need to rehash or consider the past. No need to reinvent the wheel. These students are dialed in to a familiar axiom about the nature of wisdom: the older we get the less we know. A dangerous syllogism begins to ferment in their minds: if living begets knowing, and knowing begets confusion, then knowing as little as possible has its rewards. Unfortunately, their ignorance sometimes breeds arrogance. "What kind of pedantic charade," they wonder "is this guy creating by suggesting that I embrace humility through spirited learning and thinking?" When I quote Da Vinci and say that the greatest of all joys is the joy of understanding, many of them probably assume that I've lived a thoroughly sheltered life.

No, this is a different brand of intellectual arrogance. It's not the conventional arrogance of ages past in which a highly intelligent or well-read student stridently asserts, "I already know all this." It is an arrogance that now says, "I don't need any of this. It's all pointless for where I'm going and who I'm going to be." This is the genus of arrogance that one of my finest students told me was so prominent in my classes. Ironically, we were at a dinner in which he was to receive an award for winning an essay competition. He had written a brilliant essay about the prescience of Lincoln's political thinking and its keen insights into the problems of modern politics. He leaned over to me and whispered, "I want to thank you Mr. Adams for all the help you gave me. Just so you know, not all of us are cynical."

"What do you mean?" I asked.

It was then that this gem of a student stretched across his empty dinner plate and softly released a diatribe against his classmates. He explained in painful detail the color and content of their cynicism. Young people, I had always and falsely assumed, are supposed to be the idealists and the protectors of progress. Almost all political and cultural revolutions are led by young people and take place in countries with bulging youth populations. Young people are supposed to be dressed in the poetic armor of optimism. Cynicism is not just parasitic to society; it is death to a classroom. It ends the conversation. It renders the potential of dialogue useless.

I am beginning to feel tragically unhip and ill suited, perhaps, to teach some of these students anything. Many of them fail to share my basic assumptions about the human condition, though they would never phrase it in such a manner. I believe that to be human is to be born in a state of abject helplessness with nary a resource in our young quiver to preserve ourselves. We cannot feed, warm, or protect ourselves. As The Axe would say, we are "incomplete." Yet as we mature and begin to fend for ourselves, we discover a form of incompleteness that is the legitimate child of our moribund nature, one that is rooted in an intellectual and spiritual longing for wholeness, one that finds expression in a mind that realizes time is running out for each of us, no matter how young or old we may be. A mind that understands its own finitude begins to question existence and yearns to find meaning with whatever sands of the hourglass remain. We struggle to master the quagmires of love and friendship. We eventually begin to understand that to live well requires that we act on more than mere instinct and for more than just ourselves. We begin to think about the types of human beings we wish to become. We ponder the great goal of fusing life's two biggest questions: what should I believe and how should I live? Tragically, it is at this universal juncture of life, where the classroom can and should be decisive, that many of my students arrogantly assert that they don't need the help of their teachers. They don't need history and literature. They don't need religion and science. They don't need the mind to facilitate the proper and highest actions of the body. They might not know it, but they are screaming, "I am complete!"

Maybe students now learn through osmosis or come equipped with all the answers mankind has struggled to obtain for thousands of years. I really don't know. But I doubt it. What I believe is occurring, sadly, is a wholesale rejection of the Socratic project of learning. Students don't feel particularly incomplete. There is no yearning to be whole, no quest for wisdom or self-knowledge. No acknowledgement that Aristotle was right in saying that "all human beings desire to know." The angst that so often plagues young people is not as prominent in their everyday lives. I have even begun to ask myself, "What do they know that I don't?" They seem supremely self-sufficient. Perhaps longing and angst do not command the primacy in the lives of young people as they once did. Perhaps these perennial fixtures of the teenage condition are no longer in vogue.

It is easy for me to forget that most of the students I teach are genuinely kind and interesting young people. My frustrations are very specific and far from omnipresent. Sometimes they become zombies, sometimes they are zealots, but most students, most of the time, are refreshingly pleasant on a daily basis. They are easy to smile, quick to laugh, and capable of wearing many hats. Most of the students I teach have strong loyalties to the high school they attend. They possess unwavering faith that tomorrow will always be better than today and are never shocked when things go right, only when they go wrong. They might not know or admit it, but they believe in a thoroughly American view of the world. To them, human rights are universal, opportunity ought to be abundant, and equality should be found in every facet of society, from legal and education systems to quality health care for all.

My frustration is not that all my students are zombies

and zealots every day. My frustration is that the frequency of these attitudes is on the rise. The sentiment of the British political scientist Sir Ernest Barker is fundamentally lost on them: "Outside the cottage, I had nothing but my school; but having my school I had everything."

Professor Martin has now been retired for twelve years. I don't think he ever knew my name. I did absolutely nothing in the class to truly distinguish myself. I don't know what he is doing or even if he is still alive. I certainly hope that he is. I wonder if he still remembers the fleeting moments of his career or if he chooses to focus on better days and better classes. I wonder if he, too, thought of us as zombies and zealots. I'm sure he felt the way that I feel—that what we study is important, that education should be formative, that those who sit listlessly are missing out on something vital and significant.

I think of his last class and I cannot help but gaze thirty years into my own future. What will I say as the clock ticks closer to the end of the last period, on the last day, during the last year of my career? Will I call them "diffident" and anticlimactically exit the classroom? The students who will one day sit in those desks won't be born for another twelve years. By that time my oldest daughter will be four years older than I am today. When that final bell rings and the fullness of the room quickly evaporates into a grim emptiness, I will probably walk over to the window on the west side of my classroom and look out at the courtyard which is occupied by a single beautiful tree whose leaves are in the midst of blossoming into a striking spring green.

What will I remember as I stand at the window, staring at the students shuffling onto school buses for a final time?

I hope that after forty years of serving as the sole hierophant of Harvey Auditorium 308, I leave the classroom wanting more. I hope my departure leaves me craving the conception of more academic progeny. I hope that I am only pulled away by the allure of a world filled with new places, different people, and infinite possibilities I still want to explore.

But most of all, I hope I can proudly declare that I finally learned to make enthusiasts out of zombies and thinkers out of zealots.

INTERLUDE TWO
CORN-COB ON THE DOG
(FEBRUARY, 2005)

I was not going to lose this contest of wills to a two-year old.

Our elder daughter, Lauren, with a steadfast determination normally reserved for either Olympians or the mentally deranged, decided that her days of sleeping in a crib were behind her. We had already lowered the mattress to as low as it would go, and still she was able to swing her leg in a pendulum-like manner to catapult her small body out of the crib and onto the carpet of her bedroom. Once liberated from her crib, Lauren would prance into my bedroom; she was rather fond of my bed, of course, and with the bionic acuity of a superhuman two-year old, seemed determined to replace me as the rightful occupant of the right-hand side of the marital bed.

After a few nights of Lauren using my cranium as a

bull's eye when stretching and contorting in the midst of her slumber, I decided it was time to assert my paternal power against my only child. I went to our second home, Babies-R-Us, where I was thrilled to discover a wondrous invention called a "crib tent." A crib tent is a tent that is placed on the top of a crib so that a toddler is incapable of crawling out of it—think baby jail meets a mosquito net.

Certain that victory was mine, I fastened on the crib tent, placed my daughter in it—whose hysterics began before it was even zipped up—and waited for the Ferberization gods to eventually visit her. She screamed for a few minutes and I returned to my bedroom eagerly anticipating a rare interlude with the television.

To my great surprise Lauren walked in the room as if nothing had happened and said, "Hello Daddy!"

My wife and I looked each other with grave stares of consternation, wondering, of course, how we had been out-witted yet again. It turns out, the fold between the end of the zipper's arch and the exterior of the crib tent is not so tight that a two-year old finger can't nudge itself into the fold to unzip the tent. It took Lauren less than five minutes to figure it out.

So the next night I came with a rope.

I weaved the rope through the zipper and double (or triple or quadruple) knotted the damn zipper to the wooden columns of the crib. Lauren immediately tried to unzip the crib tent and this time—yes this time!—her twenty-eight year old father had outsmarted her. Her histrionics would have been mistaken for demonic possession in medieval times, but despite the endless stream of tears (one never knows the prodigious nature of tear ducts until having children) and the screams that seemed to be eternal in nature, a perverse part of me was aglow in the triumphalism of the entire episode.

After a few minutes of delicious silence, I got greedy and wanted visual confirmation of my parental conquest. My walk to Lauren's room was the last moment I ever allowed myself to entertain the deception that I was completely in control of my own children. Instead of silence, I was greeted with a quiet but steady cadence of giggles that can only be described as more than devious but less than demonic. I quickly opened my eyes to discover the source of infantile humor.

It is not hyperbole to say that what I saw took my breath away. Lauren had soiled her diaper and decided to remove her diaper filled with feces and wipe it on the wall outside of her crib. Its enigmatic fixture on her cream walls struck me as a perverted but possible example of early 21st century avant-garde art.

Lauren knew she would have to be cleaned up and that her scatological display would be rewarded with a removal from the torturous crib tent. We ended up purchasing a bed for her the next weekend. Since then I am never surprised when my children manage to finagle their inchoate will into an undeniable reality.

This episode was one of many hurdles I encountered on the confused but wondrous thoroughfare of parenthood. I had been walking on it for two years since Lauren's birth when, in the fall of 2004, I was thrilled to discover that it was about to become even more congested. My wife and I received a call from our adoption attorney informing us that a full-blooded sibling was due in March and wanted to know if we had any interest in pursuing a second adoption. We were jubilant.

But our second daughter, Emma Kate, didn't fully cooperate. She was born two months premature and had it not been for the miracles of modern medicine and the heroics of everyday doctors and nurses, I doubt very much that she would be with us today. I am not sure if all parents who have a second child automatically assume that the second will be a carbon copy of the first one. I did and I was terribly wrong in this assumption.

Lauren was not an easy baby, but things got easier around the time we put her in her own bed. Emma, on the other hand, decided to lay low, seducing us into a lull of parental complacency by being a relatively easy infant. It was almost as if she had deliberately decided to be different, to show us an altered and more exotic side of a three-year old than what her older sister had demonstrated to us. We used to call Emma "Happy Baby." We had long abandoned this moniker, however, by the time she reached three.

I can remember this period in Emma's life and, to be honest, I don't even smile in retrospect. Midway through a family cruise to the Caribbean she decided that she was going to wear the same dress, every day, night and day, no matter what we happened to be doing. After two days of the most God-forsaken screeching that had to sound eerily similar to the torture chambers of the despotic world—all this, mind you, because we simply wanted her to wear a different article of clothing—we were emotionally and physically exhausted, drained of any capacity for anything resembling fun. Emma is freakishly double-jointed all over her body. It took both of her parents' physical and emotional strength to wrestle her out of this dress and into pajamas or another piece of clothing. When we look at pictures of this family vacation, you can easily tell if we had yet to encounter the tsunami that was Emma Kate Adams. All of the pictures from the last few days of the vacation are of haggard and wounded souls, trudging through the waning days of their vacation with a little girl wearing the same dress that got progressively dirtier as we approached the twilight of our vacation.

Similar bouts of hysteria were annoyingly common the following school year if we attempted to dress her in something that offended her three-year old fashion sensibilities. I should have known I was in trouble when, at a very young age, Emma decided she would only drink from a purple Sippy cup. I guess pink and red weren't good enough.

She is always good for a laugh, though.

When Emma was in pre-school she decided that she was a comedian. She always resented her older sister getting to ride on the big, mythic yellow school bus every morning while she had to be dropped off at her pre-school. By March, her behavior at the bus stop had reached a humorous pitch. On a cold and somewhat foggy morning when all the parents and school children were silently standing around waiting for the bus to arrive, Emma loudly announced, "My Daddy likes to exercise naked!" (For the record, I am fully clothed when going to the gym.) The next week on Saint Patrick's Day she decided to pinch one of the dads at the bus stop for not wearing green. When a four-year old extends her arm to pinch a grown man one can imagine where she ended up pinching him. Last year, while at the local mall, Emma decided she wanted to eat lunch at a famous fast food chain, Hot Dog on A Stick. But first we had to decipher exactly what she meant when she said, "Daddy, I want to go to Corn Cob on the Dog!"

There must be some elegant Darwinian theory that explains why new parents almost universally have trouble remembering what in the world they did with their time before having children. To this day I cannot remember what life was like for my wife and me before it was regimented by the rigors of soccer practices, Girl Scout meetings, nightly homework, and a slew of parental minutiae that stridently sets the parameters of normal living in my household. I can't imagine my life without Lauren's strident determination and

Emma's outrageous expressions.

There are now moments in my life when I look at my children and feel a love that can only be described as transcendent, unbounded, utterly ineffable and impossible of containment by the shallow vessels of human words. I don't know if every parent feels the way that I do, but I certainly hope that they do. I know I have reached middle age because my dreams now have more to do with their lives than my own. I want them to feel inspiration unfettered by the modern temptations of cynicism. I want them to feel a pure and magnificent love that gives birth to a vision of life defined by its devotion and service to others. I want them to feel interconnected, to feel the exhilaration of youthful euphoria but simultaneously to be grounded by a quiet and private wisdom.

When I was younger, I certainly loved my parents and my siblings. And yes, I am fortunate enough to have "fallen in love" with an extraordinary woman who I am honored to live my life with. But the love I have for my children strikes me as a force unparalleled in the realm of human experience, almost as though my emotion for them requires an entirely different grammar of communication. It is not enough to merely say that I love my children. What fatherhood has taught me about teaching—what I hope has transformed me into a better and more sensitive teacher—is that almost every student sitting in my classroom has someone out in the world who feels about them the way that I feel about my own children.

Such a dashing realization encourages both a sensitivity towards the students I teach and a diligence to give them everything I would want given to my own children. We Americans like to say that a high quality education is a right, but everyone knows that truly magical teachers are as rare as lottery tickets. I am no lottery ticket for my students, but I know that in the years since I have become a father, I now do a better job of seeing my students as much more than just the faces behind an impersonal test score. For me, my students constitute a type of family, a family of learners brought together for nine months in order to pursue a deeper principle than base self-preservation or simple material sustenance. This family has its own power structure, its own moments of delectable ecstasy and maddening frustration. Most of all, it is a family that is destined not to be together forever. Like relatives that move away from one another when they are in their youth, we ultimately spend more years thinking back on our brief time with one another than we actually spent in each other's company. It is concomitantly bittersweet and wonderful. It is an important realization to make because it forces me to understand that every day in a classroom counts. There is a never a bad day to learn, never an excuse to pass out a ditto or turn on a DVD.

One of the things both my children and my students have taught me is that I have no control over what they will remember of the time we spent together. We hope that the good lessons are cemented into the consciousnesses of our students forever and that the mediocre ones are correspondingly forgotten. But the truth is that a student from a decade earlier could just as easily recall being yelled at, or picked on, than artfully instructed. In a very odd but philosophic sense, there are thousands of "Me's" out in the world, each one the mental construct of a former student who has but a few fleeting images of our time together. This realization is a stern but steady reminder to be the best I can be every day, no matter what. Their unflattering memories of me will not note that I was frustrated with one of my children, that I was feeling under the weather, or that I was worn down at the end of a long teaching week. I don't want them to remember or believe that I could have been better, or kinder, or more devoted.

I always hoped and expected to get better at teaching as my career wore on. But I never expected my children to be the inspiration they've been. As I have aged, though, I have discovered to my great alarm that there are certain unbridgeable chasms between my students and me—some being a function of age. Others, more practically, are an outgrowth of experiences I cannot fully explain to my teen-age students. They cannot possibly understand that having children changes the nature of fear from one that is wholly egocentric ("Please, Lord, don't let me die until I have seen and achieved all that I have ever dreamed of!") to an equally mighty, though less selfish, version of dread ("Please, Lord, let me see my children grow into adulthood; let me see them enjoy the splendors of love and accomplishment; let me be there when they need me most!") Oddly enough, having children punctuates both the scarcity of time and the celerity of it. My inability to teach my students what I have learned from my own children is a good thing, though—for it preserves the future joy of self-discovery. If a teacher in my past had tried to explain to me the scarcity of time, the inspiration of parenting, or the evolving nature of human fear, I would have merely shrugged it off, confident that it wasn't important to the content of the class itself.

Parenting has given me a rich panorama of virtues that are useful in the classroom—patience, devotion, and above all, hope. But this is not a parenting tome. It is a work that is the legitimate child of my classroom frustrations; frustrations that have grown to a slow boil these past few years. They are frustrations that are powerful and poignant enough to have me questioning if I belong in the classroom for the next thirty years. I certainly hope I do. But before I can continue on there are things that must be said—for better or for worse. I must say them to my former and current students.

Above all, I need to look in the mirror and consider what I see.

PART III
SOMETHING'S WRONG IN HERE

CHAPTER VI
THE VOLKSLAUF

"Few men have any next; they live from hand to mouth, without plan, and are ever at the end of their line, and after each action wait for an impulse from abroad."
  -Ralph Waldo Emerson

Every October there is a colorful event in Kern County called the Volkslauf. Volkslauf, a German word, means "fun run" or "the people's run." This isn't the typical 5K or 10K jaunt down a street or on a sidewalk, mind you, which a local charity or business sponsors in support of cancer research or children's literacy. No, the Volkslauf is organized by the local marines and takes place on an obstacle course designed to challenge and strengthen aspiring American soldiers.

For the annual event the obstacle course is sated with wide, deep mud puddles and the course is sprayed down with so much water that it is virtually impossible to progress beyond a slow, trudging gait. Participants must use masking tape to attach their shoes to their ankles. Otherwise, their shoes will fall off in the middle of the "run." In addition to the deep mud puddles that bear more of a resemblance to lakes than puddles, dozens of walls, ropes, and motes must be successfully mounted and hurdled if one is to complete the event. All the while marines stridently scream in your face with a passion and in a manner that only a marine can exhibit. "SEMPER FI," I guess. To me, the Volkslauf represented a Byzantine maze of torrential torment from which I was unlikely to ever recover. This was an appropriate venue for many things: dread, embarrassment, and failure. The mud was fertile ground for athletes, warriors and health aficionados.

But it was not the appropriate place for a class reunion.

Yet in August of 2007 I received an email from two former students asking me if I would like to compete in the Volkslauf with them. These two young men, Michael and Kevin, were two of my favorite former students. I had come to know them well during their senior years as students in my Advanced Placement government and economics course. They also played on the junior varsity tennis team for the years I served as its coach. When they played doubles together we called them the "Asian sensations." And now they surely wanted to extract revenge for all the pushing and yelling on the tennis court, the homework and exams in the classroom.

I must admit: I was more than a little hesitant to participate. At the time I was more than a bit overweight and hadn't done a pull up—much less mounted a wall or successfully climbed across monkey bars—since I was a student in elementary school. How in the world was I going to hurdle six-foot walls and master slippery ladders? The prospect of success was, for lack of a better word, slim.

When the day of the Volkslauf arrived, I foresaw that an unfortunate comedy was about to unfold at my expense. An additional hurdle had been placed in my way by the fact that I had been up all night with a stomach ailment. I had prepared for the event in precisely the wrong way. Instead of trying to amass upper body strength for the various walls and ladders, which is what I should have done, I simply prepared by running practice 5Ks for fear that I wouldn't have the endurance to run the distance of the entire course.

Kevin and Michael were both very slim and fit. They weren't athletic wunderkinds, but they were still young and agile. I, on the other hand, always elicited stern admonishments from fitness websites that warned me of my "dangerous" BMI level. When I looked around at the other participants, I felt like I was playing a sinister game of "Where's Waldo?" Still, Michael and Kevin insisted on two goals: 1) We would complete the run together, no matter what. 2) Our goal should be to finish in under an hour. As one of them told me beforehand, "Anyone can finish if you have enough time and enough people pushing you over the obstacles. Let's push it a little."

Worse yet, Kevin's brother showed up at the Volkslauf with a camera to chronicle the event in utter, embarrassing detail. In the two hundred seventy-one pictures he took that day, a hefty majority capture an image of Kevin and Michael pushing me over a wall or pulling me out of a deep mud puddle, cajoling me to pick up the pace or laughing at the titanic hole gaping from the back of my shorts when they got caught on the very first wall we encountered. What these pictures did not capture was the propitious encouragement and joy they shared with me during my one hour of complete, unfettered hell. We finished the Volkslauf in under an hour. When I look back on the many pictures from that day a sentimental smile cannot help but creep across my face.

The next day I sent them a note with a simple message:

> It occurred to me as I looked through these
> pictures that there is no more appropriate
> metaphor for life than the Volkslauf. Life is
> muddy, unexpected, painful, but most im-
> portantly, impossible to complete without
> the friendship and love of those around us.
> As a teacher, I know how it feels to some-
> times want more for my students than
> they seem to want for themselves. If ever
> there was a role reversal, it was yesterday. And
> I thank you. I am blessed to have had the two
> of you in class, but even more blessed to now
> call you my friends. I know that for the two of
> you, the best is yet to be.

I am absolutely certain that the future burns bright for both of these fine young men. But neither of them has had a particularly easy time of things in the period following their college graduations. In August of 2008, Michael's father was tragically killed in an airplane accident. Kevin's mother passed away years earlier before he entered high school. Both of them have struggled to find their place in the world in the years following college. Kevin wants to be a doctor but has yet to be admitted to medical school. Michael has talked about joining the military, opening up a kabob stand, and trading currency, just to name a few options.

When I consider the difficulties faced by Kevin and Michael, a number of realities crystallize at once. The first is how rare it is for me to actually follow the progression of my students into adult life. Most of my former students are on life trajectories that lay hidden and obscured from my view, reminding me about the most painful element of teaching high school seniors. For those of us who teach high school seniors there is no "next year," no potential for any common future that might exist between us. As the years have worn on, this reality bothers me more and more as I find myself slouching into a melancholy state as June approaches. I mask my sadness by signing yearbooks, giving the occasional rah-rah address at the school baccalaureate ceremony, attending some of the fun senior activities where a handful of seniors go under hypnosis and act like fools in front of the entire graduating class. But invariably graduation night beckons and with it the admission that my self-deception is just that.

What I remember about my own high school graduation was how profoundly anticlimactic it felt. As a teenager, I thirsted for liberation and hounded my parents for gradual steps towards complete emancipation. Yet when the moment that symbolizes youthful independence arrived, I was left feeling that it was hollow, barren of any true substance of adulthood. I felt as though a high school graduation was the ultimate in tomfoolery. I never doubted that I would graduate from high school. The pomp and circumstance, literally, felt unmerited. The real markers of manhood, I later learned, are never ceremonial. They manifest themselves in the most unexpected of moments and places. Perhaps when experiencing the euphoria of real love or the despair of a debilitating loss for the first time. But eighteen-year-olds don't know that yet. They yearn for the sweet chasm that separates youth from adulthood and they will clutch at the most provincial of opportunities to widen it, even a humdrum high school graduation.

As I sit on the high school football field every June listening to the monotonous parade of names being read from the podium, I cannot stop the low-grade, inner agony that springs from the recognition that I will never see most of

these students ever again. There are no more opportunities
to rectify my mistakes. No more lessons to give. No more
tests to grade. The bells of the school that for so long cast a
powerful force on the lives of these students no longer hold
any regimental authority. Their new station in life is a form
of exile without the notoriety of being an outlaw. This sadness is one that I never expected when I entered the teaching
profession. The idealist in me hoped for perpetual inspiration and the realist knew disappointment would rear its
head in the course of a teaching career. But I never expected
heartache. Not for teenagers. Not during a high school
graduation.

This isn't to deny that sometimes there are students I
am thankful are now moving on. Just as the best spouses
can love each other and still need some time apart every
now and then (sometimes just in the other room, sometimes
for a day), so too do students and teachers reach a point at
which they need some separation. Even some of my favorite
students begin to wield a rather loose and spirited tongue
around graduation time. They start asking when they can
call me by my first name. I can feel their not-so-subtle clam-
or to be on a more equal footing with their teachers. They
are clearly tired of living under the protective aegis of their
high school mentors. The vortex that their senior teachers
have attempted to keep them in now dissolves into a mutual
desire for separation. There is no formal divorce, of course.
Just a diploma that decrees they can now slip into a vortex of
their own choosing.

Of the six hundred or so graduates who walk across
the stage every spring, I know roughly one hundred of them
fairly well. I spend a decent chunk of my second week of
Christmas vacation writing recommendation letters for a siz-
able portion of these hundred. I am sure some of the college
admissions committees around the state of California know

my prose intimately well. The number of former students
who stop by to say hello or write the occasional email naturally atrophies as the years wear on. When they are college
freshmen a couple dozen visit my classroom or write at
some point to tell me about their college experiences. Sadly,
however, three or four years after graduating only five or six
from each class ever keep semi-regular contact. They have
constructed lives that bear little semblance or connection
to their high school years. It's not that most of them look
down on their high schools lives. The natural proclivity for
men and women in their early twenties is to look forward
to a fully formed adult life. To stop, look back, and touch
an artifact of their teenage years does not rank high on their
priority lists at such an age. I am getting an early taste of
how the elderly must sometimes feel about a world that has
passed them by. It reminds me of the opening lyrics of the
song, "Hello In There."

> *Well, it's been years since the kids have grown,*
> *A life of their own left us alone.*

I sometimes feel like reciting the chorus of this song to
my long-departed students.

> *Ya' know that old trees just grow stronger,*
> *And old rivers grow wilder ev'ry day.*
> *Old people just grow lonesome*
> *Waiting for someone to say, "Hello in there,*
> *hello."*

While there is no doubt that I both miss and think
about my former students a great deal, I also worry about the
ones I keep in contact with. The second realization Kevin
and Michael helped me to make is to recognize how similar

their paths are with many of the former students I know. I have been teaching long enough to know students who are in their mid to late twenties. What is interesting about Michael and Kevin is that they are the typical sort of student with whom I stay in contact.

They are also the type of former students who give me a great deal of concern and consternation.

Most of my former students are very intelligent and unflinchingly kind. They are the types of people I would have befriended when I was in high school. They could be trusted with both the weight of the world or the intimacy of a friend's most private secrets. But they almost universally enter the world with a profound timidity that borders on confusion. Despite their many wonderful and affable qualities, most of them seem ill equipped to make defining decisions for themselves. They seem to be paralyzed by some alien force they can neither describe nor identify. It's not that they don't follow their self-interest: it's that they don't know how to define what that self-interest is or ought to be. It's not that they don't dream. Perhaps what they suffer from is an excess of dreams—for dreams retain the virginal and attractive possibility of a life as yet unlived.

Many of my former students refuse to choose a single path. What is most terrifying to many of them is that they have no skills or knowledge that would allow them to obtain good jobs and the promise of advancement. They are tired of school and don't want to pursue graduate school. This difficult duality leaves them few options. They have degrees but don't find their subject area interesting enough to justify further schooling. It doesn't take them long after graduation to realize that a history or English or sociology degree doesn't qualify them as particularly special in a labor market glutted with abundant BAs and BSs. Anywhere they go and any job they take immediately after college is going to be a harsh counterpoint to the libertine lifestyles they practiced in their college years. Paltry pay, starting positions, and eight-hour workdays are sure to greet fresh graduates with a ghastly thud. "Perhaps," they think to themselves, "this transition would be bearable if I could simply take some time off and just ready myself for the onslaught of adulthood that lies ahead." Many of them are repulsed by the specter of spending years at the bottom of a ladder they have no real interest in climbing.

They are so fearful of making the wrong decision that they don't make any decisions at all. Their fatigue finds no slumber in a Procrustean bed of new expectations. Many of them move home and wait for inspiration to strike. Kevin always aspired to become a doctor. Yet he is a perfect example of this timidity. He worked very diligently in college taking classes in the hard sciences and obtaining stellar grades. He obtained a job in a hospital to get some experience dealing with patients. He took the MCAT and did fairly well. He did everything he was supposed to do to become a doctor except apply to medical school. And although his example is a bit extreme, his fears are nothing different from the rest of my long, lost students who are paralyzed by the stakes involved in these decisions of definition. He naturally wondered, "What if medical school is not for me? What if I don't like it? What if I'm no good at it? If I go to medical school that means I can't do x, y, and z. I will have wasted so many years of my life. I have to be absolutely sure about this before I make a jump this big." They are so afraid of being wrong, being disappointed, or just being plain failures that they refuse to position themselves for such fates.

The tragedy of this dolorous timidity is that it robs them of the opportunity to start on the journey towards achieving their goals. If the direction they took was a mistake (if they hate their job or flunk out of med school or get nothing out

of grad school), at least they will have acquired the wisdom
of now knowing that this is not what they want to do with
their lives. They won't be left to wonder the rest of their lives
about 'what could have been.' They'll definitely know. And
in the process of discovering what it is they don't want to do,
there is a strong possibility that they will unearth what it is
they do want to do. But to make such a discovery requires
that one be on a path of some kind, not a parentally-subsi-
dized holding pattern that doesn't land until twenty-five or
twenty-six years of age.

To be charitable, I know exactly what my former students are the most fearful of. I know what it is they are running from. They are dashing away from the moment we all
dread the most in life: the moment when one has no choice
but to fully accept the enormity of personal failure, when the
gap between one's highest hopes and one's ultimate reality
is no longer deniable, a moment that cannot be softened by
the promise of new possibilities or tenderized by the gentle
prospect of hope. For those students who reject the safe seductions of a protective timidity and dare to dream big, hope
hard, and conceive of lives that subsist with a majestic pulse
of the extraordinary, there is no Volkslauf without the mud.
Avoiding the leap into the world saves my former students
from the inevitable and daunting thud that echoes from
their possible failure. This begs the question: are my former
students wise to avoid these moments of failure at all costs?
Does real wisdom at their age consist of running from the
battles that inevitable cut and demoralize us later in life?

After all, the rejection note from medical school after
spending years in pursuit of admission, the inability to find a
job in the industry of one's aspirations, or the soul-crushing
redundancy of rejection for those who aspire to write, paint,
or compose, registers somewhere between spiritual despair
and a high-velocity kick to the stomach. Why invite such a

sullen reality into our lives, they surely wager? Why open the door to the attendant self-loathing and Herculean dejection that invariably occupies the inner-cavern of one's being in the aftermath of unfettered failure?

I sympathize with their plights. I really do. And the oddity of this sympathy is that I understand it now, after a decade of teaching, more than I would have at twenty-two; perhaps my sympathy for them is the fundamental catalyst of this memoir. Let me put it this way: I love watching the Oscars, the finals of Wimbledon, and the Olympics for the same reason. There are moments during these events where perfect success and ascendant aspirations intersect for a few fortunate souls, where there is no gap between the ideal and the real. As a teacher, I know these are moments I will never experience. I can only vicariously understand them through the voyeurism supplied by the television screen. When I was a young man I assumed my time for such a grand moment would someday arrive. I certainly knew it wouldn't be a Wimbledon trophy, an Oscar or a gold medal, but I knew my moment of memorable perfection would become manifest at some juncture of life—about this I had a great deal of faith. But as the years have worn on, somewhere along the way, these expectations morphed into a high fantasy. And if I am being honest, in the back of my mind I now know that these are moments for other people, not for me. I have lost faith in myself to reach such heights. I don't even know what such a splendorous moment would look like for a high school teacher in his second decade of teaching. Maybe it has taken me a decade to realize what my former students already know. Maybe this is what it means to grow up, to mature.

Perhaps that's why I have been thinking a lot about Oedipus this summer. Watching my former students reminds me that my gold medal or Oscar rests with them. I teach them in the infancy of their lives and then must recede to the periphery of their journeys. The first time I encountered Sophocles' masterpiece, I was in my educational childhood and the play seemed both manipulative and foreign. But as I have matured, something about it rings out as vaguely familiar to me, like the simulacra of a dream that quickly turns into a moment of potent déjà vu. In my youth, the disparity between the world I knew and the world I wanted seemed like a challenge, a life's mission to close the gap between the two. Young people tend to possess a soaring and triumphant optimism because they have faith in both the reality and potency of their free will. But lately I have come to accept the Oedipal reality that, at least in the realm of teachers and students, free will is often the handmaiden of the Fates. I cannot will my students to make of their lives what I think they should. I cannot tell them what to do, which dream to pursue, which relationships are worth ending and which are worth cultivating. I cannot do for my former students in life what Michael and Kevin did for me on the day of the Volkslauf. And because I can't, there is no Oscar or trophy to be won.

The fact that I sympathize with my former students and can relate to what they are feeling doesn't mean I'm not a little disappointed by the lethargy with which many of them approach their adult lives. It leads me to ask if I am merely being a fuddy-duddy. But it also necessitates the search for culprits of their profound timidity and apprehension.

Perhaps the most obvious explanation of my former students' behavior is that they are habitués of an American generation that embrace a culture of choice. Almost every facet of modern American life is sprinkled with endless choices. Nothing makes this reality more obvious than standing behind a teenager at a Starbucks or trying to keep up with their ever-burgeoning arsenal of technological gadgetry. They can log onto iTunes and choose virtually any song, symphony, or piece of music that has ever been written. When I was a kid, we had to wait for our favorite song to come on the radio and then quickly record it on a blank tape. The entire corpus of human knowledge is just a few clicks away on the Internet. Whatever metaphor is used by the literati—the world is getting smaller, the world is flat, the world is becoming interconnected—young people only know a world where potential trumps necessity.

It is a difficult thing to tell young people that choosing a life is not like choosing a channel or a coffee flavor. Life is supposed to be difficult. There are few obvious choices or everyone would make them without regret or hesitation. And as much as I care about most of my students, there comes a point in life where you can't always keep all your options open. It's time to stop searching for the newest and the latest. Growing up means choosing. It means prioritizing. It means saying "yes" to some opportunities and "no" to others.

"Keeping my options open" has become the *de rigeur* refrain for a great many of my former students. It is both the gold standard and the holy grail of post-collegiate situational aims. It doesn't occur to them that they are slowly morphing into master virtuosos of escapism. "Keeping my options open" is, no doubt, wise advice to follow from time to time. But too often it has become a porous justification through which any and all delayed decisions flow. They have been counseled from the time they were children not to do anything that would possibly hamper their futures—drugs, pregnancy, a criminal record. It is almost as if they are still scared to act in any manner that would hamper or aid any future, good or bad.

Have I, as their teacher, added to their pensiveness? The truth is that I, too, have repeated many of the same pathetic platitudes and empty axioms that are told to young people with embarrassing frequency. We teachers often mol-

lify reality by blithely telling every student that he/she can
be everything he/she always wanted to be. But the world is
not their oyster. And no, the world is not filled with infinite
potential for each and every individual. What we should
tell them is the truth, that the choices for who they become,
what they do, and where they live are numerous and plentiful. But, to a large degree, this spectrum of possibilities
complicates the task of those perched on the plateau of adulthood. A world of choices paralyzes them in this instance.
Awareness of the possibilities merely enhances the cost of
every decision a young person makes.

    I remember I once told a history class that life, to a
certain extent, was easier a hundred years ago when a young
man knew he was taking over his father's business and
women acknowledged their domestic destiny in the rearing
of children and maintenance of the home. There is a word
for the fact that this is no long the scenario young people
encounter. That word is "progress." But with this progress
comes the recognition that for every life we choose, we
must forsake countless others. My former students refuse
to recognize this basic fact. They want to see the world, but
they also want to open up a small business. They don't really
know where their niche is so they decide to go to law school
because they claim a Juris Doctor offers them a richer menu
of choices in the future. They really love their college boyfriend or girlfriend, but they don't want to sacrifice a single
future prospect to make their relationship work. To so many
of them, committing to a profession, a place, or a person
really means not committing to a million other possibilities.
To choose is to make a Faustian compact they know they
will forever regret. They are afraid of closing the book on
so much they want to see and do. They don't want to "settle
down" or "grow up" because in their mind such action represents the entrance to a life of infinitely small possibilities.

My former students are well aware of the vastness of the playground in front of them. I don't blame them for feeling stifled by their prospects and stymied by the demands placed upon them. Can you imagine taking a child to a park filled with toys of every sort and telling the child she can only play on one of them forever? It's not that I can't relate to them. I too wonder how my life would be different had I pursued a doctorate in political science or heeded my father's wishes and gone to law school. Becoming men and women of substance requires young people to wean themselves of the narcotic fiction that they can immediately become rock stars and rock climbers, classroom teachers and Himalayan tour guides. It would be a very narrow mind that didn't succumb to occasional ruminations about the boundless possibilities of life. And yes, life can and should be a wondrous walk to take, sometimes occasioned with bouts of edification or moments of exalted joy. Most of the waves we encounter in life, however, are neither glorious nor particularly ennobling.

But that is no excuse for avoiding them forever.

Perhaps a second culprit is college itself. Many of my students attend universities with fabulous professors and beautiful campuses. UC Santa Cruz and UC Santa Barbara literally overlook the Pacific Ocean. Berkeley and UCLA have campuses that are perfectly manicured and located in exciting urban settings. The campuses possess a bevy of miniaturized meadows within which students can read, play Frisbee, or work on one's tan. (It is California, after all.) Many of the campuses have exercise facilities that would put local gyms to shame. These are often the venues where students glimpse a form of life that is ultimately unsustainable in the years following college.

During one's college years a student frequently experiences the splendorous enchantment of the life of the mind for the first time. Many a philosopher has weighed the vir-

tues of both a reflective life and a life of action and engagement. Cicero wrestled with the two. Sir Francis Bacon was a
goliath in the world of philosophy (his thoughts on scientific
methodologies helped to usher in the Scientific Revolution),
but was also a maestro in the realm of real world political
calculus, serving as an advisor to various members of British royalty. Often in the midst of reading an Emerson or a
Proust for the first time or engaging in the weighty pessi-
mism of a Schopenhauer or Diogenes, students detect a scent
of a life beyond its banal headlines. Colleges are good at
keeping the weight of the world at bay for a few years to encourage the necessary space for such an important detection.
The first time one senses it there is the sharp and unfamiliar
desire to never let it go, to stay at Walden Pond forever, to
yearn for exile from the world of routine we know so well in
anticipation of something more permanent and true, something kept alive by the embryonic palpitations of this new
wonderment and surprise. I distinctly remember the first
time my heartbeat was ever raised by the words on a page.
The exhilaration was supplied by Thoreau. It was an exhilaration I wanted to hold on to forever. The words on the page
originated from the *locus classicus* of *Walden* and seemed to
be pointing to another place, another time, another possibility for life heretofore unknown to me:

> Most of the luxuries, and many of the so-
> called comforts of life, are not only not indis-
> pensable, but positive hindrances to the eleva-
> tion of mankind. With respect to luxuries and
> comforts, the wisest have ever lived a more
> simple and meagre life than the poor. The an-
> cient philosophers, Chinese, Hindoo, Persian,
> and Greek, were a class than which none has
> been poorer in outward riches, none so rich in

inward. We know not much about them. It is remarkable that we know so much of them as we do. The same is true of the more modern reformers and benefactors of their race. None can be an impartial or wise observer of human life but from the vantage ground of what we should call voluntary poverty. Of a life of luxury the fruit is luxury, whether in agriculture, or commerce, or literature, or art. There are nowadays professors of philosophy, but not philosophers. Yet it is admirable to profess because it was once admirable to live. To be a philosopher is not merely to have subtle thoughts, nor even to found a school, but so to love wisdom as to live according to its dictates, a life of simplicity, independence, magnanimity, and trust. It is to solve some of the problems of life, not only theoretically, but practically.

Magnanimity! Wisdom! Elevation! How could a life of immediacy not seem all the more drab and redundant in the aftermath of reading about such exceptional possibilities? That is, of course, why literature and art are important fixtures of life. Hence, the sentiment of Sir Richard Livingstone who once explained, "We are tied down, all our days and for the greater part of our days, to the commonplace. That is where contact with great thinkers, great literature helps. In their company we are still in the ordinary world, but it is the ordinary world transfigured and seen through the eyes of wisdom and genius. And some of their vision becomes our own."

For many of my former students, college is the 21st century incarnation of Walden Pond where the monotonous tentacles of the commonplace cannot reach or touch them.

The distance between that hallowed ideal and the reality of starting life anew in a nine-to-five job is almost more than they can bear. They rejoice at Thoreau or Plato, find exhilaration in a laboratory or on an archeological dig, but in their hearts they know it all must come to an end. What are they to do when graduation confronts them?

The problem with inspiration is knowing what to do with it. And because so few of us are Mozarts, Mendels, or Montaignes, the insouciance of the world seems inhospitable to the allure of our collegiate experiences. Graduates often feel the agonizing disconnect between the collegiate universe of ideas and the world of practical affairs. They do not want to embrace the latter if it means abandoning the former. To merge the two, of course, is the ultimate aspiration of every college graduate. Achieving such a synthesis is rare, even for those who make their livings by writing and teaching. I remember thinking that contact with such enthrallment in one's college years was wonderful but perhaps a little bit dangerous. It would be wise to remember that Thoreau did not live at Walden Pond forever. All symphonies come to a conclusion. Art is art, not because it merges itself with the world, but because it stands aloft from the world's innumerable imperfections. While my former students frequently exhibit a timidity that is common for young people in their early twenties, what is disappointing is how long it takes them to detoxify themselves from the collegiate lifestyles they so adore.

When I talk to my own former students or read their emails, there is often a plea for advice. Many of these young people were so cocksure, so filled with faith about their own place in the world, that to witness their timidity four years later is an unsettling spectacle to behold. If someone would just tell them the "right" course to take they would happily follow it. My advice is usually simple: make decisions. Do

Jeremy Adams   211

something. Do it somewhere. Start walking down a path
of some sort. They are actually surprisingly keen to what I
have to say. Not because it is particularly original or sage-
like, but because it is an explicit directive about what not to
do. If the modern web of possibilities cripples young people
by its vastness, then they naturally and warmly welcome any
advice that closes the web just a smidgen.

Am I being too harsh on my former students? Possibly. It is obvious that not all of my former students adopt
a hesitant stance towards adulthood. Not all of them are
fearful of making defining decisions about their lives. Some
of them conquer the hesitation and fear. Some of them actually choose one of the options in front of them and jump
feet first into the world that awaits them. A former student
of mine who decided to apply for Teach For America wrote
me an email early in her senior year of college recalling my
off-handed comment about how much easier it was to make
life decisions a hundred years ago. I had forgotten about the
comment until she reminded me of it. She wrote to tell me
that as a senior in college she now saw the veracity of the
statement. She felt the weight of a world of infinite options
bearing down on her. But unlike so many of her peers, she
actually made a decision. She made the infinite, finite. She
doesn't know if she'll like teaching. She has no idea what it is
like to command a classroom of her own. I am certain that
she will succeed if for no other reason than she tends to succeed in everything she undertakes. But even if she doesn't,
she is more likely to take another leap, perhaps into another
career or a completely different mode of living like the Peace
Corps or some other agency that specializes in global volun-
teerism.

What is interesting is that despite the variety of places
they go and the array of tasks they undertake, most of my
former students who enthusiastically jump into adult life

share a number of qualities. The most important quality is the capacity for sustained hard work. It's not original or sexy. But it's true. The best students, no matter what grade they receive in the class, are those who never expect a class, a test, or an assignment to be easy. These students don't begrudge a challenge and the first person they blame for poor performance is not the teacher, but themselves. So many students simply "get by" with the bear minimum of work and effort because they are relatively bright. These students learn early on how to play the system. On countless occasions, the student who is diligent, who sacrifices time with her friends, who falls asleep with her head on her notebook receives a lower score than the student who has a knack for test taking or fast recall. The only time I really want to admonish a student is when I pass back a successful exam and the only snarky remark I hear is, "And I didn't even study." To the hard-working student who experiences less success, this is nothing short of demoralizing. I know. I was that kid.

I want to take these dutiful students aside and tell them that their day will come. The hard work. The good habits. The striving. None of it is for naught. Their disposition towards learning and towards life will serve them well when the time for early adulthood beckons. The test-taking maestros will wither in the face of new challenges. These hard workers are also the students who truly absorb what education has to offer them. They might not circle the right answer on every test question, but they have processed the information in such a way that it stays with them for a lifetime. That is why I tell my students that the same people who work hard, have a positive attitude, and really take something from the classroom are the same people who work hard and succeed in the work place of life.

Perhaps the ultimate answer is that there is no problem with my former students. The problem is me. After all, this memoir is the brainchild of a teacher who feels off track. Human lives—their contours, colors, and content—are constructed in the steady denomination of decades, not years. Like the generations that have come before them, they are afraid of losing the security and wonder of their youth, scared of failure, weary of not becoming the men and women they always dreamed they would become, even if such a dream is fuzzy, at best. I would do well to look in the mirror. I have failed to pursue some of my own aspirations, largely out of fear. I must confront this brutal reality and learn from it. Perhaps one of my former teachers is out in the world patiently wondering when I will finally do all that I am capable of doing, waiting for me to start the next great program in civics education, write something noteworthy, or make a contribution to my community that touches lives for the better. If my teachers can do me the honor of being patient as I confront my own fears of failure, perhaps I should adopt their charitable disposition towards my own students.

These thoughts about my former students have come to me slowly over the past few years. In fact, every single day I think about my former students—sometimes a little, sometimes a lot—because of two discolored plaster marks at the end of my hallway. These two marks remind me of the most outrageous episode of my teaching career. About two years ago one of my heavy-set students, who, mind you, was a lineman for the football team, made a quip about being able to run faster than me. Make no mistake: this was a big boy. But, I thought, I am surprisingly quick for someone over thirty years old. Maybe a little competition putting him in his place was a good idea.

It was a Friday in the late spring and I was sporting jeans and tennis shoes. I thought to myself it would be harmless and a little bit fun to take him up on his challenge at the end of the class period. The class wandered outside to watch us sprint down the hallway. All thirty students lined up against the wall with looks of anxious excitement.

"Whoever touches that wall at the end of the hallway is the winner," I declared. The hallway was about thirty yards long. The wall that constituted the finish line had a door in the middle of it that served as the entrance to the choir teacher's office.

"Fine," my student confidently replied.

We stood at the entrance of my classroom door. We both leaned down in a runner's posture.

A student yelled "go" and off we ran.

He was actually very fast. About halfway down the hallway I took it up a gear and felt myself pulling away. He quickly countered my celerity with a burst of his own. I could hear the kids inside the classrooms we were running past erupt with murmurs of interest. Teachers stuck their heads into the hallway to see what the ruckus was about. The dead end wall was fast approaching and I assumed that we were headed for something resembling a tie.

As we approached the wall that served as a finish line, I did what any normal human being would do. I slowed down. My football player student, on the other hand, was not normal. He was a teenage boy and thus assumed the wall could withstand a collision with a two hundred and twenty pound eighteen year old running at full speed. My mistake was to assume that he would slow down, too. But my assumption was false. In his zest for victory my student almost ran through the wall...literally. His elbow and knee were lodged deep into the wall. White, chalky drywall smattered all over the brown-colored ground. Small droplets of blood formed on the tip of his elbow.

The question of who won or lost became moot as I was already fretting the call to the office to explain what had happened. But what I remember most was the look on my students' faces as I turned around and made the long walk back to my classroom. There was a strange medley of awe, amusement, and wonder strewn across their faces. It was a look I hadn't seen in a long time. I use these two discolored marks to remind myself that the students who witnessed this humorous spectacle are somewhere out in the world. I wonder if they smile when they remember what occurred on that spring morning years ago.

My former students always believe that I want them to go on to become the President of the United States or win the Nobel Prize. But what I say on the last class on their last day of high school often comes to them as a surprise. I tell them I want the same two things for them that I want for my own children. I want them to be good people. I want them to be happy people. And I hope they discover, through whatever adventures await them, that these are two sides of the same coin of life. What they achieve beyond that is wonderful. It makes me feel good to know that perhaps I had a microscopic hand in their successes. But I want them to have lives that are full of connections to other people and other causes. I want my students to think big thoughts and feel mighty emotions. I want them to live lives free from the regrets bred by poor decisions and timidity. I hope they do not become apostles of the ever-popular and corrupting influence of absurdism; the dangerous idea that life can never possess any meaning beyond the fleeting pleasures of the moment. The irony is that my connection to all of them has saved me from ever feeling that my life is absurd and unworthy of grand ambition.

My hope for them is not a spotlight, but a candle that flickers with the ebb and flow of their choices and paths.

I plan on competing in the Volkslauf again some day, hopefully sometime soon. When the weather changes and the tree leaves begin to darken, I am always tempted to

pick up the phone and call Michael and Kevin. But something in me holds back. I think it is my own dream of how
I want the next Volkslauf to unfold. Life is not a sprint, it's
a marathon, and there is no reason why the seventeenth or
twenty-sixth miles can't be better than the first or second. I
close my eyes and can only hope that when the time for the
race does come, I will be better prepared. Maybe this time I
will be competing with a doctor and an entrepreneur by my
side. Maybe all of us will be able to enjoy our time in the
mud, knowing that the finish line only means something if
there is a little pain along the way, knowing that no wall was
ever mounted alone, knowing this time I conquered my fear
of the Volkslauf and they found their own path to the finish
line.

I hope.

CHAPTER VII
A PEDAGOGY OF PROPOSITIONS & PRESCIENCE

"The spirit of democracy cannot be imposed from without. It has to come from within."
   -Gandhi

Every four years I organize a large and boisterous party on the night of the presidential election. The parties are well attended and I strongly encourage a jovial sense of partisanship amongst the students to make the night more interesting: Republicans wear red, Democrats sport blue, and Independents search their wardrobes for a purple article of clothing.

The parties are always popular for the students and their parents. I am both encouraged and enchanted by the youthful enthusiasm my students exhibit during these qua-drennial soirees. I am not sure if they relish these evenings because we treat them as quasi-sporting events—candidates replace sports teams as the objects of our rooting and yelling. (Instead of scoring a touchdown or hitting a homerun, a candidate wins Florida or captures the twenty electoral votes in Ohio). The students who are already eighteen proudly display their "I Voted" stickers and seem to keep them attached to their shirts throughout the day. The students who have to watch the election from the sidelines actively resent their exclusion from the process, sometimes protesting their discrimination in humorous ways: insulting the intelligence of their eighteen-year old classmates, questioning the justness of the twenty-sixth amendment, complaining that they shouldn't have to wait four more years.

Sometimes the candidates and propositions I personally support end up winning. Sometimes they don't. But no matter the outcome, I always feel good about my students at the end of these evenings. Lecturing students day after day about the separation of powers or the concept of selective incorporation is one thing. Watching them exalt or despair over the results of a modern American election, however, is a better buoy of their potential for future civic-mindedness. My hopes for their political futures are modest. It is true that I am a big fan of the Hamiltonian sentiment that "ambition is the ruling passion of the most noble minds." And yes, it would be wonderful to see some of my former students run for office someday or become famous Washington politicos. But at my core I simply want my students to be able to watch and digest the news, to read a newspaper, or actively observe a political debate. I want them to take citizenship seriously.

When elections roll around they take note. But in the meantime, i.e. the other ninety-nine percent of the time, the entire notion of passionate and informed patriotism seems to elude many of them. They are suspicious of patriotism as a general principal. My ever-evolving rationale for this lack of nationalistic zest runs the gamut from the status quo (they disapprove of the current projection of American power in the world) to the historical (they have never had to sacrifice an iota of anything to enjoy the extraordinary standard of living they have always been afforded).

My questions proliferate as the years go by and their apathy intensifies: have they assumed a European mind-set which views patriotism as but a short step away from the 20th century nationalism that sewed the seeds of bellicose policies? Do they know American history so well that they understand not only the movements that were fueled by high idealism—The American Revolution, The Civil War, World War II, The Civil Rights Movement— but also those policies and actions of the government that don't look as idealistic under a history professor's microscope such as the failure to broker an agreement with the Indians, the heavy-handedness with which we dealt with Latin America at the turn of the century, the deft employment of realpolitik during the Cold War as the United States befriended anti-communist dictators like Pinochet, Trujillo, and the Shah? Do modern students have such a masterful grasp on the tools of mass communication that they have adopted a global perspective on citizenship? Or, is the American system so thoroughly imbibed into the immediate consciousness of America's youth that they cannot conceive of a system that does not enjoy our level of prosperity and opportunity? Have these factors converged to recast patriotism as a virtue from a bygone era? Is patriotism now as passé as chivalry?

My students will tell you that they love their country. But the outward markings of affection are often missing. Their patriotism is lukewarm, at best. There is no deep urgency to remedy the wrongs of their country nor is there a stentorian pride to defend and promote what is laudable. If they believe in "American Exceptionalism," they would couch this belief with the caveat that all nations are exceptional "in their own way." This lack of patriotic fervor is not

endemic to either of the two major ideological traditions. I
have tepid Republicans, lackadaisical Democrats, and half-
hearted Independents. They are only seventeen and eighteen
years old, after all. At this age they tend to closely mirror the
political tendencies of their parents.

As I am unfortunately apt to do, I take their political apathy somewhat personally. While I would like to be
sophisticated in matters of politics and public policy, I have
a fairly conventional political pride in the fact that the rest
of the world is advancing at an unparalleled pace largely as
a consequence of embracing American ideas about markets,
pluralist democracy, human rights, and the rule of law. If
America has failed to live up to its highest ideals, shouldn't
students, at the very least, see it as the responsibility of their
generation to close the gap between the ideal and the real?
Shouldn't they be eager to accept the mantle of responsibility
for adjusting and refining American ideals to confront the
challenges of their own age? Instead, I witness an alarming
level of complacency and tautological reasoning: America
will be successful simply because it is America.

I used to believe I could overcome this interest deficit
by electrifying my students with fascinating anecdotes about
historical leaders, inspirational political quotes, or the occasional meaningful discussion about their place in the broader narrative of American history. I would emphasize with
great vigor and bravado the distinctive quality of America's
founding era and the personalities that fueled it. I would tell
them to take out a $1 bill and look at the Latin phrase under
the Masonic temple: *Novus Ordo Seclorum* (New Order of
the Ages). I explain that the formation of America was a
new order of the ages because it broke away from the monar-
chical traditions of divine authority. It was a new order because it was a hybrid of democratic sentiment and republican
governance. It was a new order because political authority

was now grounded in the consent of common people instead of the tenuous bloodline of a nation's leaders. It was a new order, alas, because it was the first country to be founded under the guise of Enlightenment ideas and, as de Tocqueville eloquently phrased it, "born free" from the bellicose tendencies of feudal Europe. I tell them about the extraordinary physical traits of Washington (his stamina to say up for days, his ability to supposedly throw a rock over Virginia's famous Natural Bridge), the eclectic mind of Jefferson (his gravestone lists his three grandest achievements, none of which included being president of the United States), the daunting task of Madison leading up to the Constitutional Convention (how to reconcile the vastness of America with the fact that, historically, democracies and republics only thrive in small, homogenous societies), and the contributions of Adams, Hamilton, and Franklin. I don't ignore the personal failings of these leaders nor do I deify them into gods. But I do emphasize the extraordinary nature of their accomplishments. Even more, I want them to understand that the contributions of these men and women from ages past still play a pivotal role in the privileges they enjoy. Such knowledge, I hope, will empower them to question their own duties and responsibilities to future American generations and will encourage them to use the political process as a means of evoking progress for their posterity.

What is exceptional about the students who sit in my classroom is that they have a chorus of prescience on their side. They shouldn't need my anecdotes or endless prodding. Unlike previous generations whose challenges were suddenly foisted upon them, my students must recognize that their generation will require more than just simple leadership—their rise and fall will be built on the capacity for finding reservoirs of political heroism. My students will have to solve the addiction to entitlements that are financed through massive borrowing from foreign governments while we funnel over a billion dollars a day to unstable petro-states that are either quasi-allies or explicit enemies. These students will be saddled with a national debt and unfunded liabilities in Medicare and Social Security that has so much generational imbalance that former CBO chairman David Walker toured the country to sound a wake-up call about the coming peril in our nation's finances, a problem that he calls a "demographic tsunami that will never recede." The coming fiscal cataclysm is so profound that "the United States will face debt burdens in the future that would make third-world countries look thrifty." Add to the mix the fact that no one knows what global terrorism, autocratic aggression, or religious fanaticism will look like in thirty years and you have a world that is in desperate need of heroism and sacrifice.

Talking about our problems, of course, is the first step in solving them and I, as their teacher, am supposed to be the verbal lubricant. But politics is no different than any other fixture of life—we only want to discuss that which we find interesting or important. Cultivating a genuine interest in the political process is the surest safeguard against the prospect of tyranny. Students who hold more than a passing interest in politics will not be seduced by the promises of modern day sophists and the ambitions of dangerous demagogues. They will be able to detect the differences between genuine leadership and empty oratory. Or so I hope.

But on a deeper level, there is a special burden that all civics teachers must acknowledge when teaching American students. It is a burden that the English, math, or science teacher does not bear. In fact, this burden goes to the heart of what it means to be an American. Understanding this burden and appreciating its importance has required me to think hard the last few years about a number of decisive questions: How can American society solve its problems if it cannot learn to have a calm and rational conversation with itself? What are the dangers posed to the civics classroom when it is polluted with cynicism and apathy? What can a civics teacher do to remedy any of the maladies of America's political culture?

None of the traditional flags of national identity are used in the United States to yoke it together into a single and coherent nation—not race, religion, or language. As the great Robert Penn Warren, author of *All the King's Men*, correctly observed in *The Paris Review* in 1956, "America is unique among nations because other nations are accidents of geography or race, but America is based on an idea." America purports to offer a new brand of national identity that is distinct from the old-world orientation of feudal Europe and the *ancien régime* of the European aristocracy. The essence of being an American, what Jefferson grandly labeled "Americanism," is a matter of civic belief. FDR put it succinctly: "Americanism is a matter of the heart and mind; Americanism is not, and never was, a matter of race and ancestry."

It is true that most citizens are Americans by virtue of their birth. But just as Christians often speak of being "reborn" as a way of denoting a growing spiritual awareness of a deeper and more transcendent reality, so too must a re-birth occur in every American if they are to fully appreciate and understand the meaning of their national identity. To further the analogy, we civics teachers at the secondary and collegiate level are the high priests of America's civic religion. Our lectures are certainly not sermons and they are not seasoned with religious content, yet there is an ideological tincture to them that cannot be avoided. Unlike other civilizations that rely upon a common history or race for its communal zeal, America's national identity is forged by a belief in what Lincoln called "a proposition," a proposition that was given a voice in the *Declaration of Independence*. But this is no ordinary proposition. It is a grand assertion that self-government is born of an innate human rationality and dignity; starting with the birth of America, political legitimacy would no longer rest on the inherited political authority of an aristocratic monarchy or radiate from the ecclesiastic dogmas of the church.

It is humbling to realize that it is I who must help cultivate the civic "heart and mind" of my students so that they fully understand this "proposition." I am their portal to Madison's constitutional genius and Jefferson's political optimism, their path to Washington's leadership and Lincoln's political cunning. That their initial brush with America's defining propositions will likely transpire within the walls of my classroom is a sobering realization that cannot help but give me great pause.

If our defining proposition means anything, it means that my students cannot rely on their ethnic background or family history as a means of establishing their own national identity. Democratic citizenship requires certain habits of the mind that can only be nurtured and cultivated in the American classroom. Democratic citizenship demands a certain level of civic esprit. Becoming an American is both simple and difficult. It is simple because there is no preexisting historical narrative one must subscribe to. This is why immigrants tend to make good American citizens. Democratic citizenship is difficult because a nation built upon a "proposition" must ensure that all of its citizens understand what this proposition means and what it requires.

That is where I come in.

Yes, this proposition seems straightforward: "All men are created equal." What is not so simple is understanding the classical democratic and republican roots of this proposition, especially in an era which tends to ignore the contributions of Ancient Rome and Ancient Athens. It is not simple to explain the complex machinery of government—checks and balances, the branches of government, federalism, a complex and often conflicting political culture—that ensures this proposition is heartily enforced. What is not so easy is elucidating the evolution of this proposition, from the brio of Jefferson's *Declaration* to the reformulation of self-government in Lincoln's *Gettysburg Address* to modern incarnations of this proposition in the battle for civil rights. This proposition has bolstered a political culture that champions intellectual and religious liberty, bountiful due process protections, and a system of political parties, interest groups and elections. It is a tall task to teach such a bulky and important subject to American seventeen and eighteen-year-olds in the course of a single collegiate quarter or high school semester.

For most students, my class is their first exposure to America's unique political origins and culture. It might even be fair to argue, as Jefferson did, that the embryo of a thriving democracy rests in the American classroom. Asking questions is often more engaging to the students than teacher pontification: Are we a nation of rugged individualists who come together to protect rights and pursue self-interest or are we one nation pursuing a common destiny? What is the proper balance between the competing and overlapping powers of state and national governments? Was America intended to be an activist government that favors the political virtue of equality or was American government intended to be limited in its scope so as to maximize claims of individual liberty? These questions manifest themselves in a dialogue concerning a multiplicity of subjects ranging from modern day problems to the intentions of the Founding Fathers.

It is this dialogue that is the true source of America's political vitality. Getting my students to participate in it is the essence of civics education.

This dialogue doesn't merely occur in the chambers of

Congress. It takes place at kitchen tables, in classrooms and universities, on editorial pages, and between private citizens. A nation's consciousness is slowly refined over time so that what is controversial to one generation is commonplace to the next. One wonders what the next generation will think of abortion, homosexual marriage, and the proper balance of commercialism and environmentalism. It is so obvious to our 21st Century minds which side had the better argument during the American Revolution, the Civil War, or the Civil Rights Era. Such clarity, however, tends to elude those who attempt to solve the modern problems of energy, education, or America's place in an advancing world. And yet, the genius of our system is that, over time, even the most controversial issues tend to be resolved around a broad consensus forged in the plebiscitary afterglow of an informed and animated national debate.

This is why one of the most pernicious aspects of modern politics is the idea, promoted by those of all political stripes, that most of the issues we face have "common sense" solutions. The truth is that governing a country as diverse and complex as the United States is a daunting task for any representative institution. Easy solutions to difficult problems rarely exist. Difficult problems are only solved through informed and difficult debate, not petty and cheap sound bites. Citizens should not expect fast solutions to difficult problems that often build up over decades of neglect. Arguing for common sense often obfuscates the true nature of a pluralistic democracy. Democracies, by nature, are conservative. They are slow to act. They tend to preserve the existing system of laws and institutions unless a crisis demands drastic change. Jimmy Carter was talking about energy independence over thirty years ago. The push for broader access to health care is now entering its third decade. It took Pearl Harbor to bring us into World War II and 9/11 for most Americans to even learn about a man named Osama Bin Laden or a terrorist network called Al-Qaeda.

Solutions might be "common sense," but the process of enlightening and informing the passions and viewpoints of the public is in no way simple. Monarchies are efficient. Democracies are messy and arduous. That is why Lincoln believed that genuine leadership doesn't merely solve problems, it elevates and instructs public discourse: "...He who moulds public sentiment, goes deeper than he who enacts statutes or pronounces decisions." That is also why Churchill declared, "Democracy is the worst form of government except for all those others that have been tried." No historic surveyor could possibly study the central disagreements of our nation's history and come to the conclusion that democracy achieves efficiency by appealing to common sense.

This difficulty of confronting problems and marshaling consensus is actually a helpful reality from a government teacher's perspective. It highlights the centrality of debate and compromise as the hallmarks of a successful democracy. Difficult problems help students to understand that social consensus and national progress do not materialize from sour partisanship, the ten-second sound bite, or trite bumper stickers that aim to vilify national leaders or offend fellow citizens. Progress in a pluralistic democracy is the result of a national conversation that is honest and straightforward about the complexity of the issues we face. That is why genuine leadership embraces and acknowledges the necessity of nuance. When partisans embrace a politics of ease that denies the difficulty of the problems we face, it is poisonous to civic discourse because it abruptly ends the dialogue. Why talk, citizens wonder, when the other side is so clueless and bereft of "common sense?"

Perhaps this is the seed from which political cynicism grows. If leaders and citizens can't rationally discuss important issues, perhaps skepticism is the proper response to the machinations of modern American democracy. The political apathy of young people is nothing new. The ratification of the 26th Amendment was an act of justice (young people who die for their country should have a voice in its policies), but it was not a panacea for eliminating political cynicism in the hearts and minds of young people. What is ironic and dangerous is that the population most affected by the public policy being written today are the very people who are the least likely to have a voice in shaping it. We hear calls to "Rock the Vote" and P. Diddy (or whatever his name is this week) warns us to "Vote or Die!" Merely telling them they should read more books, hold more discussions, watch more newscasts, and become more politically engaged is about as rote as telling them to brush their teeth and take out the garbage.

But still, it needs to be said—especially in light of the activity I like to give on the first day of my university class. My college courses normally range in size from fifty to eighty students. They are often set in large lecture halls and the unfortunate truth is that I rarely get to know many of my students particularly well. All of the students took a high school government class, but that unfortunately doesn't guarantee that they know anything. I tell them this is just a diagnostic test and that it's just for fun. But this a bit of a white lie. I am curious to discover what the students know. And in almost every class the sad answer is, "Not much!"

I start off with a picture of our local congressman.

"How many people know who this is?" I innocently ask. Maybe four of five out of seventy raise their hand. I then post a picture of the latest starlet to make headlines—Kim Kardashian, Jamie Lynn Spears, and Lindsay Lohan have all made appearances during this introductory activity. Universal recognition and broad smiles greet the posting of their picture. I then show a slide of one of our senators from California—Barbara Boxer or Dianne Feinstein—who everyone comically guesses is Hillary Clinton. I then go back to a picture of a celebrity the paparazzi currently adore—someone young, wealthy, or trendy chic. Almost all the hands go up signaling universal recognition. They know Snooki of Jersey Shore but not Governor Christie of the state of New Jersey itself.

What am I to make of this, exactly? It can surely induce either laughter or tears, depending on how one chooses to look at the situation. No matter how I respond, however, I am left asking a simple question: what types of citizens do we want taking part in the national conversation about the central issues of the day? Teaching government demands the careful distillation of something American political thinker Jean Bethke Elshtain calls a "democratic disposition." FDR was right. American citizenship requires both the head and the heart.

The most expedient path towards the head and heart of my students is to encourage them to revere their nation by fostering habits that ensure its maintenance. Aristotle understood the centrality of education (*paideia*) in renewing forms of government: "That which most contributes to the permanence of constitutions is the adaptation of education to the form of government. The citizen should be molded to the form of government under which he lives."

Some commentators have unfortunately likened civics education to nothing but a watered-down form of modern American indoctrination. America is not without its national myths, the cynics tell us—its own examples of an American *Aeneid*. Washington never told a lie. Lincoln grew up in a log cabin. FDR ascended to the presidency from the restrictive position of a wheelchair. You get the point.

I have found it to be vogue and perhaps a little too fashionable in the West to be hypercritical of one's own country, especially if that country happens to be the United States of America. But there is a stark difference between indoctrination and exposure to civics education. That difference is that American students are taught to revere a system that champions an objective critique of civil society through the freedom of innovative thought and the flowering of individualistic expression. We love our national heroes only insofar as they are praetorian keepers of the American creed, not because they claim a "mandate from heaven" or are sanctioned by "divine right" to rule. Students are free to question the wisdom and thought of its founding heroes and current leadership. If anything is indoctrinated in American democracy, it is the beauty of individual thought and inventiveness. We teachers of the democratic faith are not stealth Machiavellis, manipulating our students to believe in political ideals without merit. Indeed, if there is a valid complaint about America, it is that we have not always lived up to the high idealism of our founding documents. This complaint is not a condemnation of these ideals but an affirmation of our frailty as human beings. It does not speak to the wrong-headedness of civics education, but instead bolsters the case for it.

Instilling a democratic disposition requires teachers to explain and illustrate that freedom of thought is a catalyst for achieving a richer understanding of the world and one another. Tolerance is not served when a student simply sits at his/her desk thinking nary a thought. Genuine tolerance means a citizen will have the abundant opportunity to listen to all sides of an issue before adopting a conviction about it. Possessing political convictions is not tantamount to having political opinions. Generally, everyone has an opinion. But a conviction can be defended. Convictions are forged because a citizen has done the hard work of thinking, reading, and most importantly, discussing an issue with fellow citizens.

American educators would do well to remember the link between democracy and education that was first elucidated by the Socratic Greeks over two millennia ago. It is no coincidence that the Greeks who made a radical break from the political and epistemic systems of the past gave us both democracy and Platonic philosophy (as opposed to oligarchy and *mythos*). After all, a different way of living required a different way of thinking. The legacy and gift of the Greeks was the projection of the human mind as a tool for impersonal, detached, disembodied inquiry. No longer were humans to be the playthings of anthropomorphic gods or the brutal Fates. Progressive scientific enterprises, flourishing art forms, and spirited disagreement characterize a society that knows how to freely partake in the exchange of conflicting ideas and viewpoints. An objective mind, therefore, is a mind unclouded by the fog of bias and perspective. An objective mind, most importantly, is a mind that can partake in rational discussion about the highest goods in life. Socrates may have wanted to talk about Truth, Beauty, and the Good. But I guarantee anyone possessing his intellectual nature could just as easily discuss civil rights, taxes, and defense policy. Socrates could have held a spirited discussion on these matters of national concern because he had the intellectual capacity for free inquiry and enthusiastic debate, a capacity that must be the ultimate aim of all democracies in the free world. The Greeks were not romantics about their critical aptitude for free inquiry. Objective thinking is neither a tribunal of certainty nor a keeper of hidden wisdom. It was Greek democracy, after all, that ultimately put Socrates to death for corrupting the youth and for impiety. Democracies, it turns out, are not entirely rational. They can just as easily be ruled by the passions of their leaders or manipulated by the appetites of its citizens.

There is a second pillar of the democratic disposition in addition to forming convictions: civility. Students are excellent at modeling this pillar of ideal democratic citizenship. I have never seen a student shout down another for his or her beliefs. Sometimes an opinion will elicit a loud and vociferous response, especially when we are discussing hot button issues like war, abortion, or taxes.

Real civility, however, means much more than simply letting someone else have a turn at the podium. The civility that teachers should aim to cultivate is one that not only tolerates other citizens' viewpoints, but, most importantly, considers if they are true.

My students are willing to do the former but stridently eschew the latter. The result is a stale and static classroom. They tend to have the same opinions at the end of the year that they did at the beginning. There is a soft narcissism at play, a narcissism that is truly the mark of our post-modern zeitgeist, as though my students believe that everyone in America has the right to be right. They live and breathe in an educational universe of right and wrong answers. But in civics there are no multiple-choice tests. Many of them just assume that I consider my opinion to be the right opinion and mimic it accordingly. A panic splashes across their overly analytical faces when I ask them for simple opinions:

- Should we be in favor of same-sex marriage?
- Should we increase drilling for oil within our own borders?
- Should speech be limited if it denigrates an entire class of society?
- Should public school teachers be paid on a system of merit?

Democracy thus requires a community of learners who never stop learning. A community of learners is democratic by nature because it is underpinned by a spirit of equality that each perspective is valid and worthy of explication. The mistake often made by my students, however, is to confuse the equal opportunity to speak with the radically egalitarian position that all opinions are equally worthy and true. The temptation to add a consonant voice to the chorus, to pause when others pause, to resist the colorful contribution of a dissonant voice is always present. But the jury of history often exonerates the dissonant voice, the voice shrouded in the fog of minority opinion.

I spend my days nurturing the potential of a hundred future democrats so that they know how to confront these problems. They are, arguably, the most fortunate human beings to have ever walked the planet. They are free and healthy. They possess a standard of living that most historic kings and emperors could never have imagined. But they suffer from the delusion of luxury—a delusion that seems to stem from living in an era of American hegemony. This cycle of success breeding sloth is nothing new in the annals of history—just ask the Romans, the English, the Spanish, or any other hegemonic power that falsely assumed their civilization was insulated from the forces of history. Lincoln believed in the power of tragic events to renew the animating principles of a country. History reminds us that war is more natural than peace, wealth is the consequence of sacrifice, and freedom is a delicate gift that is never enjoyed by the bulk of mankind.

Our blessings require both keen understanding and passionate stewardship. They do not come to us by accident but have been delivered through the sacrifice and crucible of American generations before us. Many of my students never question their blissful fortune. To them, peace, freedom and opportunity are as natural and permanent as the fixtures of the stars. They have great faith that the formation of their political orbit will never change. Fostering classrooms that possess an urgency of purpose seasoned with workmanlike inspiration is no pedestrian calling. My job is to teach them why their faith requires more than just belief, but weighty and substantive sacrifice. My job is to remind them that their time to become political Atlases is not distant, but near. My job is to hope for the best by nudging them towards a view of what's possible and desirable on both an individual and societal scale.

My job is never to apologize for my passion even when it makes me a spectacle in their eyes.

And finally, my job is never to lose faith, to always believe that a singular voice can become a chorus, a chorus can become a cause, and a cause can become the catalyst for putting civility back into civilization. Teaching and learning civics is an opportunity for all of us to reflect on more than just the place of America, but the powerful idea of America itself. Learning civics helps us to remember that history is not static but fluid, and that the time to redirect the waters of civilization is now.

CHAPTER VIII
FULL CLASSROOMS & EMPTY SELVES

"To doubt everything or to believe everything are two equally convenient solutions; both dispense with the need for thought."
    -Henri Poincare

I used to chaperone the Winter Formal and Spring Prom. Not anymore.

I went to these dances as a high school student. I attended many a fraternity party as a college kid. But nothing prepared me for what I saw as a teacher.

The term "dirty dancing" evokes images of highly seductive dance moves, obviously reminiscent of sexual activity itself. But seductive is not the same thing as lewd or licentious. When watching the dance moves my students display at these dances, I am reminded of the Supreme Court's early and infamous attempt to describe obscenity: "I know it when I see it." Their dancing is not simply seductive or tinged with eroticism. In fact, there are times when the fleshy orb on the dance floor more resembles a bacchanalian circus than a high school dance.

It's not that I expect them to line dance or do the two-step. I am not a townsperson from *Footloose*, for goodness sake! But what I observe during these dances is not dance.

I know, I know. Teenage sexuality is nothing new. When hormones rage and curiosity blossoms, teenagers are going to experiment with their own sexuality. It is the same with every generation and there is no use in decrying the decadence of the present generation. Right? In the interest of avoiding being both highly judgmental and acutely sanctimonious, I suppose I should simply shrug my shoulders and ignore the entire spectacle. Indirectly, I suppose, that's what I do by refusing to attend. Some of my colleagues will happily take tickets at the door or hand out punch or bottled water, but refuse to go anywhere near the dance floor.

I remember attending these dances as a high school student. I wasn't much of a dancer back then but there was nothing surprising or shocking by the behavior of my classmates. I chaperoned the Spring Prom my first year as a teacher and remember having a good time watching my students enjoy the music and weather (the prom that year was located on the top of a parking garage). I distinctly remember that when everyone would jump up and down in unison it would shake the entire building, which made me understandably nervous.

But there is something different and unique about their behavior at these dances in the past few years. Beyond the vulgarity of their moves and ephemeral nature of their partners, what is most striking is the complete lack of any embarrassment suffered by the students. Sexuality, for them, is not to be guarded by the pulse of either the sacred or the private. There is no shame engaging in behavior that, traditionally, is associated with the most personal and private aspect of a human being's life and psyche. It is one thing to share one's excesses with peers; it is quite another to ostentatiously do so in front of the teachers of the high school sponsoring the event. I know my students behave differently outside of the room. To deny this obvious reality is the apex of naivety. But hiding poor behavior is—at the very least—an implicit acknowledgment that a standard of behavior exists that ought to guide us in our outward conduct.

Aren't my students afraid of revealing the most intimate part of themselves to their teachers and strangers? Aren't they afraid of revealing that part of us that is more than brain and biology, more than tissue and flesh? This mysterious part of human classification goes by many names. Scientists, philosophers and theologians have much to say about this basic reduction of being—a being that all cultures in all times seem to recognize in one form of another. In *The Theory of Moral Sentiments*, Adam Smith calls this "the man within the breast." Christians call it a soul, Hindus an atman. Descartes thought this essential, eternal part resided in the amygdala portion of the brain. Students who reject any category of moralization—who feel amusement when they should feel shame—behave as if such a part does not exist. They seem to be saying that the voice in your mind is an illusion. It's not real. There is no "you," "me," or "I" upon which to graft any taxonomy of ethics. My students are truly "empty" "selves" in the most spiritual and existential sense of the two words.

I once mentioned my disappointment to one of my classes. The reaction was one of nervous giggles and knowing glances. The sensation I experienced as their teacher was one of being on the outside of an inside joke, as if I just didn't "get" what they all understood to be true.

It has taken me many years to finally "get" it. Or, at the minimum, to formulate a hypothesis about what is plaguing my students and my classroom. Indeed, I would have been a dreadful doctor. Not because of my aversion to blood and all things clinical, but because I am slow to correctly diagnose a grave problem. The genesis of this memoir stems from a problem that is critical, perhaps even fatal, to the aspirations of the American classroom. I have the unsettling suspicion that there is a schism separating me from my students that is more complex and nuanced than the standard annoyances that plague American classrooms.

At first, I attributed my teaching malaise to be an ever-widening generational schism between my students and me. I keep getting older, yet at the outset of every school year my classroom is populated with confident seventeen-year-olds ready to conquer their final year of high school. I was ready to blame my classroom problems on the decadence of American culture, which has stealthily supplanted the mores and values I aspired to promote in my tiny corner of the world. But these problems are, at best, peripheral. There are teachers in every generation ready to make the same accusations of their students. Instead, my quest to find a deeper, more explanatory and penetrating root cause of my teaching travails sent me on an intellectual odyssey I was not fully prepared to make.

I consider myself to be a decently educated high school classroom teacher. Nothing more. I am no scholar. I'm not an expert in anything, per se. Had I lusted for the mantle of expertise I would have stayed in school and spent years of my life in deep study on a narrow intellectual question. I would now have a Ph.D. and be working at a university, if I was lucky. In summary, I was woefully ill-equipped to make the proper diagnosis about the malady which has tormented me these past few years.

Like a philologist trying to decipher the hidden meaning of an obscure text, I have attempted to discern the underlying force that seems to annually propel my students into a slow, low-impact collision with me. It is a curious collision because my students never seem to be injured by it. Almost all my former students would be shocked to know that there was ever any strain or tension between us. They would think back on our time together and rightfully conclude that I seemed to enjoy teaching them. They would also be correct if they believed I had genuine affection for a great many of them.

No, the schism I have spent this summer trying to understand never masked itself in the veneer of anything explicitly adversarial or aggressively antagonistic. No yelling. No referrals—just confusion and emptiness on my part when they leave my classroom for the final time in June.

In the wake of a great deal of thought, reading, and consideration—not to mention mountains of anguish, confusion, and frustration—I am firmly convinced that there are certain uncomfortable truths one must ignore if one is to pursue the greater ideal of being a good teacher. I have ignored these truths for the better part of a decade; yet, unfortunately, in the act of this denial I have fortified myself into an adversarial posture towards my students that is just as much my fault as it is theirs. The uncomfortable truth is that the fundamental problem of my classroom lies in the divergence of world-views between my students and me. A Herculean clash of covenants exists between us about a great many things—about what it means to live, to grow, and to become an educated human being. At first I assumed this was merely the common problem of a teacher seeing nobility in education in the face of students who naturally see school as merely as a necessity. But even this problem has deeper roots that go far beyond conventional divides.

In regards to most of the important issues of life—love, joy, family, faith, patriotism, hope—education possesses the capacity to grant us further illumination. To believe in the ubiquitous need for education in all avenues of life repositions it out of the classroom and into the wider world; such an expansive view of education spurs me to hope that my students will always be students, even when they are no longer children. In short, I hope my students eventually conflate learning with life. These beliefs, which go to the core of who I hope to be as a teacher, have never served as a prolegomenon to the content of my courses. These beliefs are mine. But they are not, in any way, the subject of what I teach. Wise teachers are guarded with their own opinions, thoughtfully avoiding the desire to cultivate cadres of students who think as the teacher thinks. For years, I naively believed that my students would eventually find their own convictions and forge them in the light of their own educational and life experiences. After all, classrooms are cerebral dressing rooms within which students try on some ideas while taking off others. I give them an array of wardrobes. They decide what to wear.

But what happens when the classroom is no longer the place for such grand projects of personal transformation? My worry and angst is not fueled by what my students think, only by their refusal to believe that some thoughts are better or more worthy than others. It doesn't matter if we are talking about wisdom in world history or tax policy in a government class. The learning experience is in a perpetual and eternal holding pattern as I wait for my students to seek nourishment from one of the many options put in front of them. I have become something I truly deplore, a caterwauling waiter who thrashes about in fury because he never receives the tip he has worked so hard to win, a discordant malcontent standing in front of a classroom asking, begging, pleading with them to decide which dish they prefer.

Are these frustrations—the dancing, the dogmatically

utilitarian view of education, behavior that belies a belief that shame is a passé emotion—interrelated in any meaningful way? I think so.

The postmodernism that began in Europe in the late 1800's largely contained itself to small pools of academic thinkers and the intelligentsia of society. By the 1960's, the British and American counter-cultures helped popularize notions of personal morality and replaced talk of virtue with the friendly parlance of "values." Morality no longer existed as an external reality upon which the individual had agency to obey or disobey. This counter-culture and its love child of inside-out morality were largely a product of university movements and other places of higher learning. My argument—my decade-in-the-making discovery—is that in the fifteen years since I was in high school, this hearty but unknowing embrace of postmodern moral relativism has trickled down the pedagogic chain and now ensnares the hearts and minds of high school students. They have no understanding of how thoroughly they are under the influence of a world-view that situates them into an adversarial posture against their teachers, especially those of my ilk.

At first, this discovery was not empowering in the least. It was debilitating, leading me to sulk in private or throw mental temper tantrums on my drive home from work everyday. I was no better than a vituperative child who wouldn't eat because his parents wouldn't let him eat chocolate for breakfast. This discovery was not an act of merciful understanding on my part, as it should have been, but an arrogant and potent constellation of judgments hurled at my innocent students. This discovery allowed me to blame my students, to shirk my own failures and insecurities, to self-righteously conclude that my students and their world-views were so different that a bridge could never be built between us. What I needed to understand was that the

danger of postmodernism is not that it is or is not correct
(heaven knows a simple high school teacher does not possess
the gusto to weigh in on that debate), but that students did
not realize its bizarre impact on all the other opinions they
purport to possess.

Perhaps this explains why students desperately want to
befriend their teachers. It always hurts their feelings when
I tell them that I am not their friend. I make a sustained
effort to be friendly and jovial, encouraging and kind. But
being friendly is not the same thing as being a true friend.
Friendship requires a different type of dynamic, a dynamic
built upon a foundation of perfect equality and trust. But the
teacher-student relationship is wholly different. At its core,
the teacher-student dynamic must reject the relativism they
crave because it asserts that the classroom is a place to convey ideas and concepts that come from people who declare
to know things, who have attained some measure of knowledge, who claim through their subjectivity to have perceived
something that is objectively true. The teacher knows this
and is thus the link between the ignorance of the student and
the material that needs to be mastered for their betterment.

Clever students often ask, "Why are any of us any more
privileged in our perspectives than the rest of mankind?"
Why does Plato know more about virtue? What does Rousseau really know of human nature? What makes Dostoevsky
an expert on guilt? Some minds, we teachers must respond—scientists and artists, writers and inventors—have a
privileged perspective because of what they have experienced
or, in some instances, because of their soaring genius. Some
people have thought hard and studied diligently in order to
climb out of the dark abyss of ignorance. It is the height of
youthful arrogance to put oneself on the same level as a Dar-
win or a Wiesel, a Tolstoy or a Buddha, merely because we
cling to the cliché that all opinions are equally valid, merely

a construct of a subjective perspective. I have never been to the Galapagos Islands. I have never meditated under a tree for over forty days. I didn't live through the horror of the holocaust. That's why I have learned from those who have.

My students misunderstand their intellectual freedom to be a banner behind which they can demand to be left alone. A friend leaves another friend alone when that's what he or she desires. A good teacher does precisely the opposite because a deeper, more fruitful freedom is one that allows the student to use her freedom to live by the highest dictates of her conscience. Socrates called himself a gadfly because he liked to pick holes in the arguments of those he questioned. He didn't leave them alone with their ignorance. His impiety was not an extension of friendship, but the employment of an aggressive dialectic to discover what is true. I guarantee that none of Socrates' victims felt like they were on an equal, friendly footing with him. Yet it was his students who came to his defense, who begged him to escape his impending date with hemlock. When I look back on the classes that truly shaped my mind and changed my life, each of them was taught by men and women whose minds I had great admiration for. They had read more, thought more, and experienced more than I had or ever would. It never occurred to me that I was on an equal footing and that the entire body of their knowledge was no better than mine. If I had thought so I probably wouldn't have listened to them. I would be the worse for it.

I have spent ten years trying to get my students to use their freedom to artfully question what they should love, how they should live, why they should believe in anything at all. I have been concerned with one objective and one objective alone: the voice inside their minds. It is the one component in the human condition that is omnipresent—family and friends may come and go, pleasures will be momentary, the celerity of life will only seem to accelerate as life advances. The central article of my faith as a teacher is that the timbre and content of this mental voice is malleable. What we learn and how we learn it can ameliorate this voice into a baritone of authority or a soprano of consonant beauty. I always believed that the mind is like any other muscle in the human body: it is affected by what it consumes and grows stronger or weaker depending on how it is used. Unfortunately, to my students, the mind and its cerebral voice are vacuous realities. They seem unable or unwilling to detect the pleasures of its improvement.

What, then, is real for my students? Not the trappings of virtue that are nothing but an ersatz and outdated form of asceticism. Not the convictions of a mind that has dared to attain some small measure of wisdom about living. Not genuine love or friendship. Not a living faith that aims at perfection. At the end of this ten-year journey, I have discovered in many of my students a postmodern void filled with only a reflexive relativism and a view that life is ultimately absurd. In such a world-view, there is only one unquestionable and authentically real element to life: their pleasures and amusements.

Much of their reality, sadly, springs from their gadgets and devices, their Starbucks, their pleasantries, the infinite supply of joyful distractions that consume them. What's real for my students is what happens outside of the classroom. What's real is the vacation from school, the exhilarating vertigo of mingling in a world that is not moral or immoral, but amoral. They would not deny the reality of drudgery, sickness, or death—the fixtures of life from which literature and science spring. But they regard these experiences as unfortunate epiphenomenal distractions. They do not believe, as the Homeric Greeks did, that difficulties possess the seeds of illumination about how one should live. These unfortunate

events are merely to be suffered through. Death is not, as
C.S. Lewis stated, a megaphone to rouse a deaf world. Suffering is not, as Aeschylus asserted, the price we pay for wisdom
in this life. Sickness is not an occasion to question one's life.
And work is nothing but a modern master, the last patina of
slavery from which there is no liberation.

What this means, of course, is that most of my students
unknowingly subscribe to a radical subjectivism in which
no objective standards can ever be known or imposed. This
subjectivism has a rather egalitarian spirit about it that is the
source of its almost universal appeal. To say that there are
objective and knowable truths is to suggest that some people
understand these truths while others do not. This requires
the admission that some human beings are wrong in their
opinions and flawed in their behavior. My students would
never voice such a belief for fear of being labeled "intolerant"
or "close minded." Again, my students are unquestionably
civil and put a premium on comity both in and out of the
classroom. If there is nothing that is ultimately knowable,
then we are all equal in our ignorance. This appeals to many
of my students who champion egalitarianism as the *summum
bonum* (greatest good) no matter the cause or social setting.
The upshot of this belief is a metaphysics of the soul in which
the highest good of human life is not excellence or virtue,
but merely rugged autonomy itself. The seven deadly sins
all focused on spiritual and physical excesses of the self. The
only sin my students perceive, however, is the sin of unjust
restraint. Why condemn their dancing? Why condemn
anything at all? By what right do I, as their teacher, pretend
to know more than they do about the proper way to conduct
oneself?

Surely religion is the last refuge from this onslaught of
watered-down nihilism. Right? Despite the fact that most
of my students are somewhat religious, they tend to pref-

ace every religious opinion with the assurance that this is "only my opinion." They are so fearful of suggesting that anybody is wrong about anything. This fear leads them to a ridiculous religious proposition in which they actually believe in a metaphysic reality, but one that is created and colored by what each individual already believes. In such a scheme atheists find eternal darkness when they die, Christians see Jesus, Hindus achieve moksha. Not only are we free to search for truth, they inadvertently argue, but we are the makers of the ultimate reality we are in search of. This creates a world-view where man is stratified into a god himself—an anthropomorphism in the highest degree that makes Narcissus look humble by comparison.

Students who attempt to square a post-modern world-view with a circular Christian piety make religion sound more like an insurance policy than a genuine covenant for living. In a God-centered existence, human beings ponder their possibilities of Perfection or Salvation in the context of helplessness; reality is the creation of a force beyond our own making. We are left with questions: Why am I alive? Who or what created me? Are there eternal consequences for temporal actions? There is a subtle declaration of powerlessness and humility in the asking of such questions. But students want control. They want choice. They want it to such an extreme they are willing to become their own gods—creators of their own eschatological fates. In their zest to be both egalitarian and tolerant, they clutch to a Me-centered universe, a universe in which my students decide what behavior they want to indulge in and search for a religion that justifies it. They don't ask what is true, they merely consider what they want. They don't want any form of objective truth, they want to create their own version of it. They want the divine yet they also crave the libertine. There is no sense that an objective reality should intrude upon their subjective wants or desires.

Oddly, my students enthusiastically embrace the relativism of Nietzsche but reject his commandment to transfigure authentic narratives of living out of the ashes of a godless world. Nietzsche called the West's monotheistic tradition "the long lie" because it forged an unstable and vacuous horizon for man to get his moral and aesthetic bearings. Empty selves affirm the lie but do not want to forge anything in its place. My students take the half of Nietzsche that hollows out the soul but ignore the half that fills it in. Liberation from the "long lie" carries with it the necessity of finding a soulful ballast of some kind. As a teacher, my hope is that my students strive for orientation. I hope they use their educations to lay a foundation for living impassioned lives. My job is not to make choices for them. My task is to ask the important questions, to give them a menu, to make them understand the stakes involved in their actions and convictions. Many of my students, however, resist the recognition (or creation) of any horizon because they believe there is nothing worth believing or constructing.

Unfortunately, this view of life makes the quest for education eternally ambiguous. Education can be useful. It can even be interesting. But for those who believe in nothing, it cannot be ennobling. Even Nietzsche, the great patriarch of the postmodern world-view, looked at the void of life's emptiness and decided nonetheless to affirm that life was worth living. If there is anything that the Christian and the nihilist can agree on, it is that life should be lived with passionate involvement. For Nietzsche, life did not have to possess any inherent meaning in order to justify enthusiastic participation. In fact, the only meaning that can be constructed is one that is chiseled from the enormous block of suffering that life affords us. It is not petty amusement that fills the void. Indeed, it is quite the opposite. This is why Nietzsche

avoided alcohol and adored mountain climbing; suffering
is the only portal to feed man's hunger for meaning. This is
also why Nietzsche found enchantment with the Greeks—
not the Socratic Greeks who he deplored as overly rational,
but the Homeric Greeks who witnessed the traumas of life
and formulated "horizons" of meaningful struggle. This is
the task of what Nietzsche called the "Superman": to affirm
an existence that is empty and barren by constructing one's
own horizon of meaning and purpose. All moral orbits and
horizons are man-made, he argued, and one orbit cannot be
canonized as any more worthy or true than another. Thus,
Nietzsche answers the fundamental existential question of,
"What should human beings do with the burden of time?"
They ought to become supermen and superwomen wielding
their absolute autonomy to bend reality to their will.

As Nietzsche comments in *The Use and Abuse of History*:

> This is a parable for every individual among
> us. He must organize the chaos in himself by
> recalling in himself his own real needs. His
> honesty, his more courageous and more gen-
> uine character, must now and then struggle
> against what will be constantly repeated, re-
> learned, and imitated. He begins then to grasp
> that culture can still be something other than a
> decoration of life, that is, basically always only
> pretence and disguise; for all ornamentation
> covers over what is decorated.

My students, however, are not unfettered Nietzsche-
ans. They do believe in the existence of moral absolutes, but
these absolutes are grounded in the sphere of political rights,
not individual behavior. The only universalism my students
subscribe to is imbued with a social and political milieu. As

individuals, my students demand total freedom to create
their own private sphere of right and wrong. The values they
choose to uphold as individuals, (i.e., how they treat themselves) is exclusively their own domain. Their ethical compact is a simple one: I won't intrude or judge your domain as
long as you don't intrude or judge mine. Sobriety, chastity,
honesty, and temperance are merely personal choices analo-
gous to ordering off a menu of virtues.

Political rights, on the other hand, seem to them to be
sacrosanct and universal. My students will readily explain
for you why torture is wrong. They will eloquently reason
out why any "ism" is deplorable: sexism, racism, ageism. The
moral order that vanished on the dance floor in regards to
personal behavior miraculously reemerges when the question of political rights arises: in fact, it ebulliently shines
forth its light for all the world to see. It is simultaneously
fascinating and disturbing that my students believe in justice,
but they do not believe in virtue. They believe government
coercion and action can degrade human dignity, but personal behavior cannot. It is an enigmatic hodge-podge of
viewpoints from which to construct a muddled view of life.

I may or may not agree with their thinking, but it makes
them deliciously interesting to teach and understand.

It is, indeed, quite curious that my students have absolute, fanatical faith in the power of reason to establish how
governments ought to treat human beings. And in this faith
and understanding my students demonstrate what they are
capable of. They don't just believe in due process, equal
rights, equal opportunity, and freedom of conscience and
expression. They can marshal forth nuanced, thoughtful
explanations about why they believe in these things and why
a government that affords its citizens these rights is more just
than a government that does not. No one really believes that
the regimes of the Nazis or the Taliban stand on equal foot-

ing to those of western liberal democracies. It is not doctrinal imperialism to say so. But when the question of personal ethics returns (i.e., how an individual ought to live his or her life) the impotence of reason and the relativism of revelation quickly return to the fore.

As I look forward to another thirty years of teaching, I wonder if there is anything on the horizon that would alter the world-view of my students. Is there anything that could change their minds about the highest goods in life? The most tragic element of their world view is that it acts as an impenetrable armour, incapable of being breached by anybody from the outside. If the humanities and social sciences have nothing to teach my students about the proper way to live, then the only conclusion that can be reached is that there exists a tragic isolation to their humanity that can be neither avoided nor softened. No books, no friends, and especially no teachers, can ever save them from the fate of living utterly alone.

This memoir is the child of my struggle with the reality of such a desolate prospect. Where does a simple high school teacher turn once faith is considered to be absurd, reason is seen as suspect, and even consciousness itself is viewed as a mental phantom? In the depths of my despair on this issue, I told a good friend about some of my fears and theories. He sat there politely taking it all in.

"We all have the same frustrations," he reminded me. "Besides," he said, "they'll figure it out."

I laughed at his optimism as one of my students might haughtily laugh at me on occasion.

He turned serious.

"Jeremy, they'll have to develop a different reality or their lives just won't work. One day they will be parents, and they'll have to give their children some values from somewhere."

It was simple yet profound. Yes, "life just won't work for them." I felt better for a few moments. Perhaps he was correct. Life will do for them what I cannot and never will do. But the darkness quickly returned with a simple question.

What if they never expect their lives to work in any meaningful way?

As I began to confront the depths of my teaching demons at the outset of this summer, I wanted to know how my students' lives would ever work. This desire is what led me to seek an understanding of what has gone wrong, but more importantly, it has encouraged me to figure out what I can do to remedy the problems. To a certain degree, what I truly required was something very simple: I needed to get over myself. Enlightenment is not always reached by pointing the spotlight on the teacher. Sometimes it is about stepping out of the light long enough to discern where it has been pointing the entire time. This memoir has been a blinding light. A step back has allowed me to see that I have been standing on an island for the past three months as I have collected my thoughts and penned them for the first time. Writing is a task done in utter isolation. Even moments of insightful joy are nonetheless enjoyed in isolation. And while my frustrations are both potent and real, I must realize that bridges can be built, even to the most desolate and isolated of islands. It is a desolation largely of my own creation, a desolation that is not only the genesis of this memoir, but also a way to begin construction of new avenues and new paths, paths paved with the hopes of a different teaching future.

There are a number of lessons I must learn to implement.

The first one is that I must have more faith in my fellow teachers. Students might not engage education with the seriousness I demand, but that doesn't mean they won't in another classroom or at another juncture in their lives. It doesn't mean a future college professor or mentor won't be able to nudge these students towards a path of seriousness and understanding that they were not ready to embrace when they sat in my classroom. Every teacher has something different to offer and teachers who try to please everyone end up pleasing no one, especially themselves. Course evaluations in my college classes make this perfectly clear; two students can sit through the same lectures with the same teacher for an entire quarter and take two radically different experiences from the classroom. Education, at its best, is a communal activity. It takes an eclectic mix of minds and talents to ready hapless teenagers for the years that lie ahead. I need to be a better team player. I am not the only one with grand ambitions and frequent disappointments. I should listen more than I talk. Such corrections will hopefully lead me to a better place, a place where I do not bemoan the clay that has been given to me.

   The second and more important lesson is that I must learn to better align my expectations with those of my students. They may expect to learn something, but that does not mean that all of them expect to be changed by what it is they learn. A teacher who constantly lionizes what he teaches cannot help but come off, at times, as little more than a self-serving and self-important martyr. I should have more faith in the power of the subjects I teach. Being pedagogically pushy might prevent a classroom from passivity, but it does very little to encourage my students to become thoughtful people and passionate stewards of their own lives. Teachers can push their students, but they can never achieve for them. Achievement requires a special autonomy of the self that can never be coerced. It must flow from a reservoir of passionate commitment that only the individual student can access and unlock. I can push them towards this reservoir, but only they can take sustenance from it.

I must stop fancying my classroom as the great instauration of my students' lives. The magic of studying history and civics will be a portal to grander schemes for some of my students. But for most it will merely be a course that satisfies a graduation requirement. I must acquire enough humility to cheerily accept this reality or else I need to do something else with my life.

I do not know if I will find the fortitude to live up to my own proclamations of improvement in the next decade of teaching. But I would do well to remember that virtue is the consequence of habituation. If I want to be a different kind of teacher, I must put away my old habits and begin anew. I cannot care for my students more than I do. I cannot love the subjects I teach more than I already love them. I hope to live out my days walking straight and walking narrow, hoping to avoid the temptations of grandeur that always seem to lead me to disappointment.

INTERLUDE THREE
A SAND FALLS TO THE EARTH
(JUNE, 2010)

Almost three years have passed since I decided to use my summer vacation to channel my frustrations into a mid-career memoir. In that time a lot has changed in my life. My wife gave birth to our son, Benjamin, in June of 2010. My younger daughter, Emma, has sprouted out of infancy and my oldest child, Lauren, talks and walks like a creature rapidly rounding the corner towards early adolescence. But most importantly for the purposes of this project, I have had three wonderful years of teaching. Yes, there are bad days and the occasional student that gets on my nerves, but on the whole, I cannot help but believe that these are the years and the students that will often send me into bouts of geriatric sentimentality in the sunset of my life and career.

Reading my words from three summers ago is disorienting because they seem to have been written by a slightly different person, a person who did the exact opposite of what the great Roman historian Tacitus claimed to achieve. Taci-

tus approached history from an unbiased perspective, claim-
ing to rise above "anger or zeal" in the retelling of Rome's
victories and foibles. I, on the other hand, only seemed to
understand the meaning of my first decade in the classroom
through an animated engagement with my own anger and
zeal, abandoning in the fecundancy of that summer three
years ago any claim of omniscience or objectivity.

Is this disorientation an indictment of my feelings of
frustration? Is it a denial of my testimony of dissatisfaction?

Not at all. Their dance moves have not inched toward
any hint of decency and the dogmatism of their classroom
utilitarianism has not waned in the least. But these realities
no longer seem to haunt me the way they once did. They
are no longer illuminated by the harsh radiance of the sun;
instead, they sit quietly in the moonlight, patiently waiting
for me to come to terms with their presence in my life.

A few weeks before my wife gave birth to our son,
Benjamin, a group of my Advanced Placement students and
their parents threw a small shower for my wife and me. My
daughters enthusiastically opened the presents with a fervor
that can never be duplicated in adulthood. As we opened
presents and ate refined food, I thought back on the past
four months since revealing to my classes that my wife and I
would be welcoming a child in the late spring, right around
the time of their graduation. When I considered the behavior of my students, I could not help but suffer a sudden
and expansive sensation of astonishment, not because I was
shocked by their lack of tact at times ("Was this planned,
Mr. Adams?"), but because I never expected them to care as
much as they did.

I waited until the second trimester of my wife's pregnancy to announce the big news. Their reaction was, at
once, touching and humorous. The female students suddenly waxed emotional and the male students treated me

like I had just won a rather large and prestigious trophy, spontaneously bursting into thunderous applause as though I had scored a winning touchdown or kicked a game-winning goal. My students wanted input and information on every front—was it a boy or girl, what would we name him, which hospital were we using for the delivery? The day after I made my announcement, one class decided to hold an impromptu party by bringing cookies in the shape of a baby from the most famous bakery in town. Another class had a different suggestion for a name almost every week. One student made a habit of getting more outrageous as the due date approached, eventually settling on something close to "Santos Achilles Leviticus Jeremy Adams." I am sure my son will one day be thankful that I demurred on this particular suggestion. Emma's suggestion was shorter but no less outrageous. Within twenty-four hours of learning of her mother's pregnancy she declared that the baby ought to be named "Martin Cantaloupe."

Their treatment of me during the spring term was a curious but touching mixture of fascination, anticipation, and, I suppose in their own way, love. There was nothing arid or detached in their enthusiasm for my son's birth. And to say that I was emotionally touched by a group of students in a way I had never been before doesn't begin to approach the magnitude of my appreciation for them (and their parents). For twelve years I misunderstood my career to be a totem standing tall in defense of a singular aspiration: I wanted my students to go places (mentally and physically) they couldn't go without a substantive education, to resist what fate had given them and partake in a noble battle against the sorrows we all eventually face. I fancied myself an eclectic maven of sorts, dispensing knowledge and posing high-minded questions. And yet, my students wanted something very different during the spring of my son's impending birth. All they wanted was to be connected to something that was undeniably real and genuine and important. I have tried to connect with my students through the enchantment of books and ideas. What they taught me, however, is that sometimes we teachers must remove the regalia of scholarship and let our students see us as ordinary people with ordinary hopes and fears. Indeed, for the first time in my teaching career, the roles were reversed; I felt like I was under the microscope of my students as they watched and wondered what it was like to rhapsodically march towards the birth of one's child. They seemed to be learning, but it had nothing to do with civics or economics.

My wife was admitted into the hospital on the day they graduated from high school. It is the only graduation ceremony I have ever missed in my career. But despite my absence, I know that on a day that should have been exclusively devoted to my students and their futures, they were quietly rooting for the teacher they might not ever see again, for the teacher who had doubted his ability to ever make a difference in their lives. What I never expected was how much of a difference they would make in mine. It would be a bit extreme to claim that my students these past three years have renewed my faith in the power and promise of teaching; I never really stopped believing. I simply had doubts and, to be honest, still do. That is why there is still a temptation at times to be pensive, to become a bit unengaged with my students on a personal basis and to keep things cool and detached. It is the temptation of a man whose heart has been broken a few too many times over the years.

But despite this heartbreak, I cannot conjure a life that doesn't include my students—both in my day-to-day existence and in the memories I continue to accumulate as the years pass. I know I will neither see nor hear from most of them ever again. If most of them appeared before my very eyes at this moment, I would recall very few names. I would surely like to shake every hand and hear about each life story as it has unfolded in the years since high school, answering every what-ever-happened-to-such-and-such question I have ever had. I know, of course, that this is fantasy. It would be a scene from a schmaltzy piece of fiction saturated with acute bathos. But still, I cannot help but yearn to feel connected, to hope that I achieved something real and genuine with these students, to feel that all of the work, the frustration, and the striving added up to more than the instillation of raw information or self-aggrandizement.

Perhaps this is a natural place to conclude—with the realization that I am a good teacher who has yet to become great. I'm a teacher who intellectually understands his students but has yet to become emotionally accepting of them. I'm a teacher who has only recently realized that love of the classroom is akin to any other form of human love. Genuine love is holistic and comprehensive; it doesn't reject imperfections but understands that these imperfections are the markings of any human being or human enterprise, especially endeavors of the classroom. I must learn to love the imperfections of my students, from their off-beat cynicism and zealotry to their dance moves and college stories. I must learn to love these imperfections because they remind me that I still have work to do. After all, artists don't always get to choose the clay from which to construct their masterpieces.

As I lie on the cusp of slumber every evening, there is no order to my thoughts, no concentration, only the maelstrom of a mind in the middle of life. In the midst of this chaos, though, there is often a consonance that rises above the cacophony of mundane worries and tedious concerns. It is a consonance that is sung by the memory of my many students. While the grand class reunion of my dreams may never happen, at night, in the darkness, my former students speak to me. It is not the voice or timbre of the dead, but the unwavering hue of hope. I don't know if other people pray for me, but in my imaginings, I feel the goodwill of my former students. Such goodwill has a pulse. Sometimes it is faint, even inaudible, when I need it most in the middle of a frustrating day or in the midst of a lecture that nobody seems to care about. But in the silence of the nighttime it radiates and reassures, pushing me on like a wave whose origin is hidden by the eternal regression of the world's infinite movements.

I continue to teach, hoping the future will be better than the past. I go with more humility than I did on the first day over a decade ago. I go to the classroom because it is where I want to be.

These are modest hopes.

But they are hopes worthy of a good life. My life.

ACKNOWLEDGEMENTS

When I consider the chorus of voices that had to come together to sing the song of this manuscript, I cannot help but feel a daunting sensation of debt to every voice, critique, and criticism that led to the publication of this work.

The voices are many…but some sing louder than the rest. I owe the realization of this dream to two people, in particular. To Kim Flachmann, who made me believe that others would one day see the magic of this manuscript, who gave me the gift of literary faith, whose expertise, encouragement, and advice could fill an entire book.

But most of all, she introduced me to the ultimate Renaissance Man, Elijah Jenkins. Elijah is the fulfiller of dreams and no words can ever begin to capture my admiration of him. Our dinner at the Padre Hotel is truly one of the defining events of my life.

To Michael Flachmann, whose advice on an education essay of mine inadvertently served as the inspiration of this work. To my niece, Jane Hawley, whose name will grace many book covers in the years ahead. Her future burns brighter than any I know. Thank you so much for your editing prowess and encouragement. I hope one day to repay the favor. To Victor Lasseter, whose friendship and guidance proved invaluable along the way.

To my college friends, Eric Reuther and Scott Bookwalter, who have had to each endure over a decade's worth of sympathy pains. Thank you Eric for serving as my memory in so many instances and for being such an important pillar in my life. Eternal thanks to Scott for reading more of my words than any human being on the planet. The constancy of your conviction in my dreams is the mark of a truly extraordinary friend—you are the kindest man I know and I am better for it.

To my many friends at Bakersfield High School and in the Political Science Department at California State University, Bakersfield. Your support is wonderful but the inspiration so many of you have provided is better. So many of my colleagues are true testaments to the artistry of the classroom

To my father who taught me what a noble life is—both in and out of the classroom. To my two brothers, Howard and Will, who ensure that I never hold my head too high.

To my mother who did not live long enough to see the publication of this work and whose vivid words I remember every day of my life: "Dreams will always remain dreams unless you believe they can come true."

To the Driller Class of 2012: Thank you for taking the final step with me. You wanted to be in the book and now you are!

To Eduardo Velasquez—"The Axe"—whose influence on my life will never waver no matter how many years separate me from the vitality of his classroom.

To my extraordinary wife, Jennifer, who defines what it means to be the love of someone's life. And finally, to my children, Lauren, Emma, and Benjamin, who remind me every day what it means to live a life of grandeur.

Mr. Adams's Required Reading

Non-Fiction

The Apology, Plato
"Of the Education of Children," Michel de Montaigne
Man's Search for Meaning, Victor Frankl
The Story of Philosophy, Will Durant
"Of the Delicacy of Taste and Passion," David Hume

Fiction

The Death of Ivan Ilyich, Leo Tolstoy
All The King's Men, Robert Penn Warren
The Moviegoer, Walker Percy
Atonement, Ian McEwan
A Farewell to Arms, Ernest Hemingway